A SOBER LIFESTYLE

SURVIVING THE FIRST 2 YEARS AND BEYOND

CAROL JONES

First published by Ultimate World Publishing 2021
Copyright © 2021 Carol Jones

ISBN

Paperback - 978-1-922597-02-1
Ebook - 978-1-922597-03-8

Carol Jones has asserted her rights under the Copyright, Designs and Patents Act 1988 to be identified as the author of this work. The information in this book is based on the author's experiences and opinions. The publisher specifically disclaims responsibility for any adverse consequences which may result from use of the information contained herein. Permission to use information has been sought by the author. Any breaches will be rectified in further editions of the book.

All rights reserved. No part of this publication may be reproduced, stored in or introduced into a retrieval system, or transmitted in any form, or by any means (electronic, mechanical, photocopying, recording or otherwise) without the prior written permission of the author. Any person who does any unauthorised act in relation to this publication may be liable to criminal prosecution and civil claims for damages. Enquiries should be made through the publisher.

Cover design: Ultimate World Publishing
Layout and typesetting: Ultimate World Publishing
Editor: Anita Saunders

Ultimate World Publishing
Diamond Creek,
Victoria Australia 3089
www.writeabook.com.au

Testimonials

Wow, what a great read! It was easy and engaging. I was drawn into the story and just kept reading until the end. The book is well written, but especially I think Carol managed to find that balance between sharing her personal journey and helpful guidelines/tips extremely well, so it was real without being self-absorbed and helpful without being too technical. Well done!

**Richard Norman, Clinical AOD Manager,
Non-Government Organisation (NGO),
Brisbane, Australia.**

Carol Jones has written a book which is honest, helpful and provides an insightful look into the life of a normal woman who woke up one day and realised she was an alcoholic. As a woman who has also used alcohol throughout my life to numb my feelings and feel invincible, I could relate to her story on so many levels. I wanted to know more! How did she cope? This book will help anyone who has the disease of alcoholism, or is stuck with a dependency on alcohol to unwind and relax. Well done, Carol, on your bravery to share your story to help others, and congratulations on your achievement of staying sober despite all the obstacles you face.

**Krissy Regan, founder of Mindful Mums,
Nth Qld, Australia.**

A SOBER LIFESTYLE

A brave and honest story of the journey from raging alcoholic to teetotaller. Following Carol's simple 'rules' has given me hope that I too might enjoy a successful sober life that is not all serious, but lots of fun too. Her passion shows through with her expressions of real and raw feelings that I found very relatable, and had me both crying and laughing. This book will not only help alcoholics/addicts, but will give 'normal' people more of an understanding of the dis-ease of alcoholism.

Trevor D, 7 weeks recovering alcoholic/addict,
Wellington, New Zealand.

I have seen Carol at her lowest, and I have seen her grow through her experience. Her determination and commitment to succeed has encouraged many others to carry on 'One Day at a Time'. In this moving and raw account she doesn't hold back in expressing her feelings. This hands-on approach to a new 'normal' lifestyle offers insight and hope that things DO get better on the other side - but it is up to you, the reader, to say "enough is enough"!

Vicki Warren, former NSAD counsellor,
Gisborne, New Zealand.

TESTIMONIALS

A Sober Lifestyle, with its practical action points, will be a great resource for others on their sober journey. I will be recommending to my colleagues in the specialties of mental health and addiction fields that they add this book to their library. Reading Carol's experiences may also facilitate better understanding and support within the family unit, and avoid unhelpful, well-meaning comments that do more harm than good. Your courage and determination is inspiring!

Tania Kelly, Mental Health Nurse,
Founder of Kelly Health:
Mental Health and Addiction Services,
Mackay, Australia

Addiction, in any form, is a cruel master. Sadly, many never find freedom from its clutches. Yet in this wonderful book Carol Jones shares a story of hope; her own story of finding freedom from addiction and the devastation it was bringing to her life and relationships.

A Sober Lifestyle is a wonderful resource both for those looking for the same freedom Carol has found, and for those who want to help guide others on that path.

Jai Wright, Pastor,
Mackey Evangelical Church,
Qld, Australia.

A SOBER LIFESTYLE

This captivating book was a pleasure to read. Carol articulates hope, wisdom and practical guidance as she shares her honest, raw and very human journey from alcoholism to recovery.

As expounded very clearly by Carol, any permanent change requires continual self-assessment and action, so I particularly appreciate for those struggling with alcoholism the practical actions she suggests at the end of each chapter.

I feel blessed to have played a very small part in Carol reuniting with an integrated and more peaceful inner child, and her ultimate victory over what sadly is often a life-destroying addiction.

I highly recommend this book, and truly feel that it can be of great assistance and guidance to those battling similar addictions.

Trudy Vesotsky, *Holistic Psychology,*
Gold Coast, Australia.

I am so grateful to have been gifted a copy of this book. It's like a lifeline for me; something to keep my head above water when I'm feeling extremely frightened and fragile still finding my feet in very early recovery.

Jackie B, 3 days sober,
Sydney, Australia.

TESTIMONIALS

This book blew me away! Carol, this is phenomenal! Why? Because I get it. It had me captivated right from the beginning. I enjoyed your wit, sense of humour and the raw, real truth behind the journey of healing.

The simple action steps which I think are so imperative; in fact, it helped me reflect on my life today and take a really good stocktake (30 years later on the journey).

I'm going to share this with our Kaupapa Whanau Oranga group here in 'Gizzy'.

Forever grateful to have walked alongside you and many others in our early days of recovery. Big Hugs. Ngamihi Aroha (much love).

Kim Whaanga-Kipa, *Kaihautu-Mauria Te Pono* **Trust. (Supporting people and their Whanau affected by alcohol and drug addictions. "By Whanau for Whanau", Gisborne 2021.) Gisborne, New Zealand.**

Dedication

I dedicate this book to all the alcoholics out there,
both in and out of recovery.

Also to the late 'Big Carol', my sponsor,
quirky friend and kindred spirit.

I'm grateful from the bottom of my heart
for all your wise words in my early days of sobriety.

Thanks also for all the butterflies you've
sent me since you passed.

I know it's you! X

Contents

Preface	xiii
Introduction	1
Chapter 1: Enough Is Enough	5
Chapter 2: Rock Bottom	9
Chapter 3: Ready Set Go	13
Chapter 4: Out With the Old	23
Chapter 5: Counselling	31
Chapter 6: Withdrawals	37
Chapter 7: Outpatients	47
Chapter 8: Alcoholics Anonymous	57
Chapter 9: Group Therapy	69
Chapter 10: Your New Social 101s	77
Chapter 11: Menus and Medications	87
Chapter 12: Niggles and Resentments	95
Chapter 13: Morning Routines and Habits	101
Chapter 14: Evening Routines and Habits	107
Chapter 15: Bills, Debt and Finances	113
Chapter 16: One Day at a Time	117
Afterword	121
Feeling Words	126
The 12 Steps of Alcoholics Anonymous	128
Recommended Reading	131
About the Author	133
Acknowledgements	135

Preface

Ensuring Anonymity
Names have been changed to maintain anonymity, privacy, confidentiality and respect to both persons and organisations.

Disclaimer
Every alcoholic and addict needs to walk their own path. There is no guarantee that following the steps that I have, and still do, will work for you.

Please Note
You'll see the word '**GOD**' mentioned throughout the book. Don't let that scare you off; this is not a religious book by any means. Turn GOD into an acronym for '**G**ood **O**rderly **D**irection' if that sits better with you.

Sobriety is a lifestyle choice. Don't try to exercise willpower as that's just too hard and exhausting, and will undoubtedly lead you back to drinking. Instead, set yourself up for success by removing temptations, and by adopting an active lifestyle and disciplining yourself to follow simple routines.

My hope is that this book helps to ease your struggle, providing you with guidance and reassuring you that your new sober lifestyle is nothing to be afraid of, but rather something to look forward to. Use the steps and tools as your 'medicine' as you embrace your second chance at life.

Introduction

My name's Carol, and I'm a very grateful alcoholic! When I got sober back in 1993, I heard that 2% of alcoholics get given the gift of sobriety, and of that 2% only 2% stay sober for the first two years! That's a very scarily low success rate, and it's probably even way less than this because there are so many alcoholics out there who don't even know they are alcoholics!

I vowed and declared that I would do whatever it took to stay sober for that first two years, and that if I managed this I would write a book on how I'd done it, to help others do the same. It was the least I could do.

For the next 24 years I attempted to write my book, even having it on my yearly Vision Boards. But I was always getting side-tracked and distracted, allowing life to get in the way.

The book started as many 'bubbles' and ideas in my head, then progressed to untold Post-it Notes stuck here, there and everywhere, moving with me whenever I changed house or migrated overseas. On my 50th birthday in 2012, I purchased my first smartphone. I was so excited when I found 'Notes' on the phone that I headed one up proudly with 'Book'. I got busy typing by transferring all of my Post-it Notes onto

A SOBER LIFESTYLE

my smartphone notes. I disposed of all the scraps of paper and felt very proud that I had now organised everything in one place.

I still kept procrastinating though, as I had so much to share that I didn't know where to start. Then in 2016 my smartphone died and I lost all of my notes! I was devastated! I beat myself up, telling myself how useless I was; if I had just written the damn book already I could have saved so many lives! I bought a new phone and every time a great thought, idea or inspiration for the book popped into my head I'd type it in 'Book' notes again, and also write it on paper and Post-its just in case my new phone 'sucked the kumara' (NZ slang for when something dies).

I was getting nowhere. What's that saying? "The definition of insanity is doing the same thing over and over and expecting a different result!" Such a fitting quote for an actively drinking alcoholic, but this one was in recovery and stone cold sober! I might have been booze-free for over 20 years but still insane in so many other areas.

I resigned myself to never getting the book written and sort of gave up. I carried on with life, but always there was this nagging voice in the back of my mind, like Jiminy Cricket sitting on my shoulder, both poking and chastising me at the same time, zapping my energy emotionally.

Twice a year, on every New Year's Day and End of Financial Year, I would revisit my goals. Writing my book would always jab me in the gut. I knew it was my purpose; this was why I was born. I was wasting what God had given me.

INTRODUCTION

Finally, in 2019, after witnessing so many people coming in and out of recovery, going back to drinking, going insane and dying, I decided, this is it; I'm writing this book come hell or high water! It's not for me, it's for all the alcoholics out there still suffering that it can help. I'd been given the gift of sobriety, how dare I not share it with others?

My Higher Power must have known I meant business. What do they say? "When the Student is ready, the Teacher appears." By chance I saw a Facebook ad by a publishing company called Ultimate 48 Hour Author™, and was intrigued. I went along to a half-day workshop where I met Natasa and Stuart Denman. They explained how they had helped turn other writers into published authors.

I now had real, tangible hope that with their professional guidance and encouragement I could get my book written and published by my 27th Recovery Birthday. Only 25 years late, but better late than never. Just like an expensive wine, good things take time to mature. Not that this alcoholic would know, as she sculled only cheap wine by the cask!

I threw away all my 'notes' and decided to keep it very basic and simple, as that's what we recovering alcoholics need. We tend to over-complicate everything and make life harder than it needs to be! So, hopefully you will find this an easy read - a basic plan to make your first two years of sobriety as simple as possible.

A SOBER LIFESTYLE

Note

This is a book about staying sober, not necessarily a book about Alcoholics Anonymous, although you will find many references to AA and the 12-Step Program as it has been, and still is, paramount to my ongoing sobriety.

Stick to your plan and you'll have a successful recovery.

"It works if you work it!"

Hugs to you all x

Chapter 1

Enough Is Enough

*If you always do what you've always done,
you'll always get what you've always got*
— Henry Ford.

Congratulations on putting down that last drink and picking up this book! You are about to begin the next chapter of your life, embarking on a journey saner and healthier than any of the past ones.

You're probably going through a rollercoaster of emotions right now, freaking out and scared shitless, asking yourself a ton of questions: "What the hell do I do next? What's going to happen? How do I stay sober? How will I cope? What will my friends say? What will my family say? Can I do this? Is it possible?"

It most definitely is possible. Along with many other sober alcoholics all over the globe I'm living proof of that. It's my aim to help guide you in the right direction and take some of your fear away. Don't think about anything too demanding at this time except getting yourself well.

A SOBER LIFESTYLE

Concentrate on *you*. You will need all your energy to help yourself get well.

I'll show you how I formed some simple daily habits, put in place routines and committed to an active lifestyle to keep safe, sane and sober. To start the recovery process from this cunning, baffling, powerful, progressive disease called alcoholism, we need to have a simple plan to follow. If we fail to plan, we plan to fail.

This is not about willpower. That would just be 'white-knuckling' it, gritting your teeth, grinning and bearing it; it would consume your every waking moment, zap all your energy and in the end it would become all too hard, succeeding only in reverting back to your old ways and habits. Before long the battle of the demon bottle would win again, mocking you and laughing in your face like the devil!

Alcoholism is no different from any other genetic disease or illness you would need to change your lifestyle for; just very misunderstood and with a hell of a stigma attached to it.

You will hopefully have hit your 'rock bottom', or your *final* rock bottom by this stage and be sick and tired of being sick and tired. You've gone through, or are going through, detox and withdrawal, experiencing or about to experience many different physical symptoms.

You've taken your first step, realising that alcohol has become a problem in your life and you have no control over it. Alcoholism is a genetic disease. It could be a lot worse. Out of all the 'dis-eases' out there I'm glad I got alcoholism.

ENOUGH IS ENOUGH

It's one disease that can be put into permanent remission if we do what we need to to keep it there. If you've made it this far, you really are one of the lucky ones.

You may have had many friends, family and even health professionals over the years try to tell you that you're an alcoholic, but that's of no help or value until you come to that realisation for yourself.

As I previously mentioned in the Introduction, I once heard a statistic that only 2% of alcoholics get given the gift of sobriety, and of that 2% only 2% make it sober to the first two years. But here's a thought: if *I* made it to two years and still counting, then that's 100% for a 'two percenter' ... mmm ... If I can do it, *anybody* can. That means you! Do you want it? I'm here to show you how it can work 100% for you as well.

I'm one of those lucky ones and it's my *calling* to share with you what I did in the first two years and still do today. If I didn't pay this forward it would be such a waste and so selfish of me. I've been fortunate enough to be given this amazing, incredible gift; how dare I not share it with you?

A SOBER LIFESTYLE

Three Actions:

1: Get yourself a refreshing glass of water or a comforting 'cuppa'.

2: Commit to reading this simple book to the end.

3: Remember you are not alone; now settle in and turn the page!

Chapter 2

Rock Bottom

The definition of insanity is doing the same thing over and over and expecting a different result
- Albert Einstein.

In a sleepy and confused voice she insisted, "He's not here. Go home to your girls." That was the moment, the *exact* moment, that stopped me in mid-rant and I realised I had it all wrong. It wasn't *her* that was the problem, it was *me*. Oh God, the penny's finally dropped! That was the 'lightbulb' moment! I have a problem with drinking!

It was 11:30 p.m. on a cold and chilly New Zealand evening in the winter of 1993. She was standing there with the front porch light behind her illuminating her long hair, appearing like an angel sent from heaven - or somewhere, I don't know where. I looked at her through eyes that only seconds before had been glazed over from a combination of rage and booze, and then noticed them *all* in front of me for the first time. A strong, united family huddled together in their pyjamas, the terrified children with their heads peeking out from behind their parents.

A SOBER LIFESTYLE

Him: six foot tall with thunder in his eyes and fists clenched at the ready, a strong and powerful warrior fixated on protecting his wahine (wife) and tamariki (kids) from this five-foot-two, 48-kilogram crazy bitch woman who appeared from nowhere.

Her: such a calm presence with softly spoken words defusing all the violence of the situation. Her hand stilling his, holding him back firmly and saying softly, "No, it's okay. It's all right. Just wait." Then silence.

They were waiting. I was wondering what had just happened. Time seemed to stand still. A few seconds with not a word spoken. It was a moment of clarity frozen in time. It was like something mammoth had just taken place, but no one was quite sure what. I took a careful step backwards, swaying slightly, and with right hand on top of left lightly touching my heart, I leaned forward and with huge remorse breathed sincerely, "I'm so sorry, I'm so sorry."

All of a sudden in a micro-second, a vision flashed through my mind of what I had done before landing in their front yard, in the middle of the night, totally uninvited. I had just compromised a major value. I hurriedly ran backwards the few steps to the car, and sliding into the driver's seat I glanced down at the console to where my coffee mug sat which was still half-full of cheap cask wine. I picked it up and tipped the liquid poison onto their grass verge. I glanced up at them with wide eyes and called out frantically, "I have to go!"

ROCK BOTTOM

I broke all the speed limits and road rules, 'pedal to the metal', racing home with a sense of urgency, praying that everyone would be okay. Had I even stopped to lock the door?! I begged God to please be looking over them and keep them safe until I would arrive at the house shortly, bargaining with him and promising I would never, ever touch another drop!

I skidded in the gravel driveway, handbrake sliding to a stop at the front door, stumbled out of the car and tripped up the steps. The door was locked, thank God, but also hindering my progress which was causing me to panic even more. Fumbling with the keys in the sticky old door lock, I dropped the keys, crouched down in the dark to find them; damn it door, don't do this to me now! Finally the lock clicked open; I bounded up the stairs two at a time and there were the kids, sleeping like babies, safe and sound.

I collapsed to my knees, sobbing uncontrollably. "Thank you, thank you, thank you, God." And promising again that I would never, ever touch another drop. I can't for the life of me believe I'd left the kids home alone! This madness had to stop! Right here, right now! I'd had my last drink.

Miraculously, I was now stone cold sober despite drinking all day and all night for the past 16 hours, and being continually topped-up for the past 16 years. That was what would later be referred to as my 'rock bottom'.

A SOBER LIFESTYLE

Three Actions:

1: Think back to the moment or moments when you realised you may have a problem with drinking.

2: What values have you compromised?

3: Have you promised yourself you will never drink again?

Chapter 3

Ready Set Go

Face the fear and do it anyway
- Louise Hay.

I woke up the next morning full of humility remembering the night before. I cringed a bit when I thought about my irrational behaviour, but there was no time to waste hashing it all over and beating myself up in this moment. I vowed and declared I would *never* drink again, and right now I had to do something drastic before my resolve left me and I would be right back in the hell-hole merry-go-round once more.

In an excited voice full of urgency she said, "There's usually about a three-week waiting period but we have just this minute had a cancellation. If you can get down here as quickly as possible we'll be able to fit you in!"

I parked the car half a block down the street. Oh God, I was so scared. How was I going to do this? I was so nervous of this appointment, but I couldn't cancel as I'd never get in again. It took weeks and I was so lucky there was a cancellation that day. This was my chance. I had to go, no matter how scared I was. How could I face them though? I was so ashamed. They'd judge me.

But then I remembered what an old drinking buddy had said: "They are so good, no judging; they're really nice and they helped my hubby." Gosh, he was a worse drinker than me, and way more drugs too. So if they helped him to stop for a while, then maybe they would be able to help me too.

I'd go this once and see what it was like. I didn't have to confess everything and after all, I could walk out anytime. It's not like they were going to put me in a straightjacket. Or were they? Shit, shit, shit! No, of course they wouldn't! It wasn't *One Flew Over the Cuckoo's Nest*! Oh God; HEAD, WILL YOU JUST SHUT UP!!!

All of these thoughts were racing through my mind at a million miles a minute. The only other time I felt this scared was when I was in labour. There was no stopping it then. I had no choice but to go through it, and coming out the other side with a precious baby was so worth it. And it wasn't nearly as bad as all the horror stories I'd heard. Maybe this 'no more drinking' would be okay too.

As such a melancholy pessimist, I was ever the eternal optimist; we alcoholics are definitely a breed of our own, full of contradictions and with a different set of tangled wiring in our brains! The most amazing thing was that right now in this moment I didn't *feel* like a drink! First time ever! I was so stressed out (anxious was the correct feeling but I never knew what anxiety was back then), and I realised I didn't need alcohol as a crutch! Wow, what was happening? Someone or

READY SET GO

something was looking after me. (I later learned this was my Higher Power.) Get your arse into that appointment quick smart!

I shimmied out of the car and with head down I scurried along to the outpatients alcohol and drug centre. I was told it was an unmarked black door next to the curtain shop. There it was! Whew, no one familiar saw me! I opened the heavy door and made my way up the dimly lit stairs, suddenly full of trepidation. What was I walking into here? In the past, I entered any unfamiliar situation with the Dutch courage of a belly full of piss and feeling ten foot tall and bulletproof and more like the leader of a pack of lions; I now felt like a small, helpless stray kitten. Then I reasoned it couldn't be nearly as bad as some of the situations I'd found myself in before.

There was no need to worry though; I was soon greeted by a softly spoken guy with a short beard and a friendly smile who welcomed me with a warm but firm handshake. "You must be Carol. You've come to the right place. Let's get a cuppa and have a chat."

There were a few people mingling about in the kitchen, laughing and hugging each other. One guy looked like someone I'd seen at the gym months before, but I couldn't be sure. Everyone appeared friendly and happy. After small talk in the kitchen making our coffee we headed to Norm's office, which was more like a cosy little lounge with comfy old furniture; no psychiatrist couch in sight!

Norm asked me how I was feeling. Sitting down slowly, I nervously answered, "Way out of my comfort zone and not sure of what to expect. I feel like I'm shaking inside."

A SOBER LIFESTYLE

He said, "That's natural. You're in a safe and confidential place here. Everyone is only on a first-name basis and everything you say here remains here between you and me."

He continued: "All I ask for your own benefit is that you are **Honest**, **Open** and **Willing**. That's the **HOW** of this thing working. Completely **Honest** with your own feelings and actions (the truth will set you free, however shameful, deceitful or unlawful, etc.), **Open** to new ways and suggestions, and **Willing** to try something different. You're not going to get into any trouble; what is said in this room stays in this room."

I said, "I'll try, my way's not working anymore."

So we started talking. He asked me a few questions about what led me here, and about my last 'drunk', which was last night. And what I was *feeling* leading up to and during my last 'drunk'. He explained that events and what people said weren't important, but my *feelings* were.

I didn't know much about *feelings* back then; I just thought everything was *dark* and *heavy* and I always had a sharp 'rock' in my chest. I was always so angry and hurt, and felt unloved and invisible.[1] He presented to me a large sheet of paper with hundreds of feeling words written on it.

Wow! Who would have thought there were so many different feeling words for *dark*? Sad, lonely, gloomy, shady, scared, frightened, anxious, fearful, etc. That piece of paper proved really handy through the early days of my recovery in identifying what I was really feeling.

READY SET GO

My counsellor was so easy to open up to. I was completely honest, hiding nothing. I never once felt judged, only accepted for who I was. I trusted him completely, like at some primal level I knew my life and sobriety depended on it. I started to feel really hopeful of a better, saner life and that I could face all of the celebrations, special occasions, birthdays, Easters, Christmases, New Years without alcohol.

There would be so many of these social occasions coming up over the rest of the years of my life. Not to mention the drinking as a crutch for every feeling or emotion, both negative and positive, and of course all situations, people or bosses that pissed me off!

I was feeling very overwhelmed, but I felt hopeful and at peace. It was the first time I could ever remember feeling peace. Norm was like the sobriety 'whisperer'. And I assumed that once upon a time he would have been in my situation himself and he'd come through the other side and was now helping others. So it *could* work, there *was* hope. I was starting to relax a wee bit.

Little did I know at the time that he was also the pastor of a local Christian church. I didn't learn this for two years and I'm so glad I was oblivious, as I don't think I would have opened up to him as honestly as I did had I known!

Then I came crashing down as he told me that my body was going to go through detox, and explained some of the physical withdrawal symptoms to expect and how to get through this time as comfortably as possible. I could be in

A SOBER LIFESTYLE

for a few rough days, or even weeks. Everyone experienced detox differently.

There could be cravings, headaches, stomach cramps, diarrhoea, sweating, tiredness, no energy, sleep disturbances, nausea, 'electric' fleas, screaming, writhing, mood swings, anger, fright, heart palpitations, hallucinations, paranoia and suicidal thoughts.

Naively, I thought it would be like giving up smoking, which I had managed a few months prior after numerous attempts. There would be a few days of painful, throbbing headaches and biting my lips, and maybe a bit of uncomfortable stomach cramping. I'd handle it like I did the nicotine withdrawal by eating Granny Smith apples and taking up knitting. Knit to the end of a row until any cravings subsided! I was optimistically picking out the side effects I thought I could manage and choosing to ignore the rest!

These days it's advised you go through your detox under medical supervision. Some people who stop heavy drinking can experience extreme withdrawals such as the DTs, otherwise known as delirium tremens. Sounds like a freaky name for a scary movie! Although uncommon, it can place you in a life-threatening situation. I'd never heard of the DTs back then so I went cold turkey, doing it by myself at home, not wanting to disrupt family routines. I had no time for doctors' appointments or hospital. I had a household and businesses to run. The kids had things going on and I had commitments and obligations.

I was to make sure I drank enough water to keep hydrated and eat what I could to remain nourished and keep my strength up. And to get enough sleep and stay away from stressful situations as much as possible over the next few months. Any social/drinking events I could put on hold for now, I would. I committed to doing *whatever* it took. I didn't ever want those *dark* feelings back again.

My counsellor prescribed 90 meetings in 90 days along with some one-on-one counselling sessions. The meetings could be a mixture of outpatients group therapy, unisex and women's only groups, and also AA (Alcoholics Anonymous) and NA (Narcotics Anonymous).

By pushing things around in his diary we scheduled three one-on-one counselling sessions per week together. It seemed like a lot, but Norm reminded me I promised I would be **Willing** to try something different; and after all, in the past I could easily fit 90 drinking sessions into 90 days. I would have all this free time now from not drinking, so I would need to fill it with something. I negotiated that the three one-on-ones be part of the 90 meetings. He shook his head while raising his eyes and clicking his tongue behind his teeth, and we had a chuckle. True! I committed to three months and then we would re-evaluate my situation.

A 12-week inpatient residential treatment facility out of town was offered (but that wasn't a viable option for me at the time as I was solely running the bookkeeping of two businesses we owned, and a very large home with hubby and three kids of different ages all at different schools/kindy, all with their individual after-school and weekend sports and activities). After confirming I had a supportive home environment, he agreed it would cause unnecessary hardship to my family at this time to attend an interstate rehab centre.

He gave me a list of days and times that the weekly group therapy sessions were available at the Outpatient Centre, both day and night, and also said there were numerous weekly AA and NA meetings too. I was amazed there was loads of valuable help and support available out there![2] And all free too! No excuses!! I vowed to make 'this 90 days thing' work without upsetting my family's schedule.

By the way, this was 27 years ago when there was no Internet, mobile phones or online meetings. Today it would be much easier to arrange around work, business, home, kids, etc. Although even today I would recommend the best meetings for success are the real-time ones, as in the physical meetings. There's nothing quite the same as 'bums on seats'.

Make the most of the time when your kids are napping, at daycare, kindy, school or with friends on play dates. Find a reliable childminder that you not only trust, but one your kids are comfortable with. If you don't have kids then take advantage of all the hours you're free and not working. There are many regular Facebook Group meetings, Step meetings, Theme meetings, Old-timers meetings, Newbies meetings and more. Some are even 24-hour meetings. Jump on and off Zoom as often as you need to! You might live in Townsville, North Queensland, Australia, but there's nothing to stop your favourite home group AA meeting being in Ontario, Canada!

READY SET GO

Each person is attending meetings for the same reason. You won't get on with everyone; we alcoholics have massive egos, sober or drunk! However, you will not only hear amazing pearls of wisdom and share some of your own to those that need to hear them, but real-time meetings are an opportunity to find a sponsor (more about this later) and also to develop physical relationships with people, rather than virtual. And, to get bear hugs! Most of us also yearn physical contact. Whether you choose to do virtual or physical meetings, try to have a mix of both.

My counsellor said, "Never forget your last *drunk*. Always remember how you were *feeling*. Don't pick up that *first* drink and you will stay sober. Remember you never want to feel like that again. The feelings of despair, self-hatred, self-loathing, loneliness, hopelessness, never fitting in, dark and suicidal thoughts. Always remember your last *drunk*!"

Armed with a list of meetings and appointments set, I left his office feeling confident that I could do this. I knew it wouldn't always be *easy,* but if I kept away from alcohol and did what was prescribed then I had a chance. I told myself, "You've been given a second chance at life; grab it with both hands and run with it."

A SOBER LIFESTYLE

Three Actions:

1: Decide today that you're going to get sober!

2: Make an appointment with an outpatients or AOD (Alcohol and Other Drugs) clinic.

3: Write down your last drunk, the situation, the people, if any, along with the *feelings* you had.

[1] List of 'feelings' words can be found at the back of this book
[2] Check if there are costs involved in your local area

Chapter 4

Out With the Old

Out, damn spot!
- Shakespeare's Lady Macbeth.

I arrived home from that meeting feeling both elated and shaky. I was so proud I had found the courage to go along. It wasn't nearly as bad as I'd imagined it to be. There was help out there for people like me. I had always been a 'lone wolf' with my problems, but now I felt a weight had been lifted off my shoulders knowing I didn't need to struggle and do this all by myself.

It was going to be a whole new way of living, completely different from what I had been used to for many, many years. I now had a plan and people to support me who had gone through it too. I wouldn't let them, myself or my family down.

Standing alone in my kitchen all I could hear was an eerie silence, like someone had died. I looked around and saw remnants of booze everywhere. I felt quite offended by the sights and smells. It was like I was seeing my surroundings for the first time as they truly were. A decrepit old museum and cemetery all at the same time. My body did a quick involuntary shiver like someone had walked over my grave. I felt like I had to clear the sight quickly before it sucked me back in.

Frantically I raced around and tipped out all the alcohol that was in the house. As I had also been a home brewer, making everything from wine to sake to cider to beer, there were many bottles of booze that went down the laundry tub. I couldn't get the caps off and corks out quick enough. I was fumbling, and in my haste the foul, sticky liquid was dripping all over my hands, down my clothes and onto my shoes, then running over the ugly old linoleum floor.

I couldn't wait until this was over to have a long, hot shower. The odours were sickening, really irritating my nostrils. It was a cross between a brewery, a winery and rotting fruit under trees, complete with a few fruit flies! I don't think I'll ever forget the smell. It's in my nostrils now as I'm writing these words. I'm feeling really nauseous and have to stop to splash my face with cold water.

I'm back now to continue writing. Wow, it's amazing the memory that's held in our cells. I just went through the same symptoms today of stomach cramping and diarrhoea *remembering* the situation that I physically went through over 20 years ago *living* the situation! Alcoholism is not a 'pretty' disease. Cynics or realists would say I must have had something bad to eat for dinner last night, but I choose to believe otherwise.

OUT WITH THE OLD

Wow, I do feel better today in 2021 than back in 1993 though. Light and cleansed, without any remnants of a hangover. Back then it was part of the *physical* detoxification process; today it's more of an *emotional* detox, or purge.

Home and business premises were on the same plot of land, with the workshop being at the side of the house. I had two offices, one in the workshop and one in the house. BC - 'Before Cleanout' - I would be brewing my booze between doing the accounts, paying the bills, making up the wages, changing the beds, mopping the floors and burping the baby.

For my wines and ciders there was always fruit to be peeled, stoned and chopped. Juices, water and sugar to be measured. I was constantly checking on the process and testing the temperature. It was one of my hobbies I was so proud of. I also enjoyed brewing different beers, especially lagers. My brother and I were a bit competitive and would compare brews and give each other tips. I have to admit his tasted better than mine; shhhh ... don't tell him!

I thought nothing of it when customers would come to the back door of the house after being sent over from the workshop by hubby to query their account or pay their monthly bill. They would stand outside, hesitantly knocking on the door, and I'd call out, "Come in, come in." There I could be found standing at the kitchen bench in some stage of brewing or testing, sometimes with baby on my hip or asleep nearby in the pram.

Now and then I'd cop a few strange looks that I chose to ignore. I had silently labelled them all 'judgemental

A SOBER LIFESTYLE

chauvinists' as brewing was a 'man' thing. It never crossed my mind that the actual *activity* itself was the unusual part, not the *'woman'* part. To me it was the most natural thing in the world to be sorting an account while brewing my beer. Multitasking, right?! Making efficient use of time as a mother and business owner. To me it was no different from baking a cake, but now I shudder to think what it looked like at the time.

Back to the cleanout. After the last drop of home brew trickled down the sink I started on the kitchen cupboards and china cabinet. Any spirits that were left over from my recent 30th birthday cocktail party themed 'Whores and Pimps' were tipped out. OMG, that was a night I wish I could forget. I remember it took me a whole day to clean up my brothel of a house after that milestone birthday of excessive over-indulgence!

I spied a few old bottles of red sitting in the wine rack up on top of the cupboards which had been given as gifts over the years. I could never drink red wine, although I did try when I was desperate. I would pour the contents of the bottle into a saucepan on the stove and gently heat it with cinnamon and mixed spice in an attempt to make it palatable. Mulled wine, right?! But I always found it just as foul-tasting to me as I thought beetroot juice would taste. Huh, a fussy alcoholic! Ever heard of such a thing?! Just spoilt for choice, I think. Down the sink it all went. Washed away. Good riddance! Out, damn spot!

It's funny that as a fit and healthy individual today, I now enjoy the amazing benefits *and* taste of beetroot juice! Every

OUT WITH THE OLD

time I currently enjoy a freshly made red juice, I quietly laugh to myself at the vision of the spicy saucepan on the stove!

I boxed up all the expensive crystal wine glasses, silver goblets, shot glasses, carafes, whiskey tumblers, jugs, schooners, handles and beer mugs. All the bottle openers, corkscrews, drink coasters, wine decanters and bottle stoppers. *And* all the ashtrays. Although I had given up smoking months before I still kept all the ashtrays handy for when my drinking buddies came over. Now that I couldn't be associating with them anymore I didn't need the foul-smelling things.

I was ruthless, like a mad woman on a mission. It didn't take long. I was really nervous that hubby would come in the back door at any minute and go mad at me. Before anything or anyone could stop me I hurriedly loaded all the boxes, bottles and crates into the back of the station wagon. I then raced upstairs for a quick cleansing shower and threw on some fresh clothes. Gosh, that felt so much better.

On the way to pick up the kids from school and kindy I stopped at the Salvos to donate the remnants and relics of a past life and then to the recycling centre and the rubbish dump. I reasoned that if everything was gone before hubby came home he wouldn't notice anything missing or see a difference.

With the car finally emptied out I felt so strong and light. It was a real statement and commitment to my new sober lifestyle. I felt like a different person and mother that afternoon when I picked up the kids. They must have wondered what was going on when I was at the school gate on time, hugged them, and then took them to the park by the beach for a play. A far cry from the norm of late, when I'd turn up after all the other kids and parents were long gone, pretending not to see their tear-stained faces peering up and down the street for me.

Unfortunately, my hubby (now ex) did notice. He thought I was crazy and was really angry at all the money wasted tipping out the booze and giving away the crystal, some of which were expensive wedding presents. I was shaking inside and feeling really intimidated by him, but I held my ground and reminded him I didn't need it anymore. And besides, it was too late now as it was all gone. I asked him, "Would you prefer I wasted all that money, or went back to all that drinking nightmare?"

That stopped him and he mumbled, "We'll see."

Of course, not everyone can do this. You might have a spouse at home who is still drinking. It's their home too. But *I* needed to do whatever I could to make myself feel safe. What I did was pretty drastic, but if you're committed to a vegan lifestyle you're not going to have meat in the house, are you? It's not so much the physical associations, it's the principles and values that come hand in hand with the lifestyle choices.

When my husband wanted a beer or wine, which he rarely did, he had to drink out of a can or a vegemite glass. It wasn't really an issue as he didn't drink in the house anymore, he just had the odd beer in the workshop with the boys at the end of the week.

OUT WITH THE OLD

My house was like a new home. I picked some daisies from the garden and popped them in a vase on the table. The kitchen now smelt fresh and looked bright and airy. To the outsider looking in it probably appeared not much had changed at all, but to me *everything* had changed and it was a pleasant place to be, both physically and emotionally.

Three Actions:

1: Take a good, honest look around your living environment from your new sober eyes.

2: Pour out all alcohol in the house. Don't give it away or save it for someone else. **POUR IT DOWN THE SINK!**

3: Clear the house of any drinking associations.

Chapter 5

Counselling

It won't happen overnight, but it will happen
- NZ actress Rachel Hunter
(Pantene shampoo TV advert).

My first official one-on-one counselling session with Norm rolled around. He asked questions that got me opening up so he could assess some issues that would need some work on. We spoke about my perception of events and my thought patterns, identifying different areas where he could see my belief patterns and perceptions were ruling my life and crippling me emotionally.

After talking heaps about different events and situations I would find myself in, we could recognise that although lots of these occasions and instances were different, my feelings were the same and I would feel like a trapped animal so would lash out. It would usually relate back to deep-rooted feelings of fear, inferiority, scarcity or feeling I had to justify myself all the time and end up being micro-managed as though I wasn't capable, both at work and home.

A SOBER LIFESTYLE

I learned about reading my feelings and what was behind them. A plan of action was decided on what feelings we could work on first over the next three months, meantime putting safeguards and boundaries in place to protect myself emotionally. The session ended with a hug. The majority of us recovering alcoholics tend to be huggers, not hand-shakers.

I was emotionally drained from the past hour but I did feel somewhat relieved. It felt like we had gotten somewhere and there was finally some structure in the chaos of my life. Although quite a bit of shame and guilt had come up, Norm explained if I was to stay sober and ease my way back into mainstream society I had to think of my emotional well-being, which in these early days meant going easy on myself. I could still feel remorseful, and at the same time I could 'shelve' any of the shameful, guilt-ridden feelings for a future session when Norm could counsel and guide me through it. There would be a time for beating myself up, but right now it was a time for self-nurturing.

I went home and lay on the bed, resting for an hour, thinking over what transpired in the counselling session. I knew we had a lot of work to do. A few soft tears fell but I wasn't afraid anymore. I'd liken it more to a state of mourning, I think, over a waste of so many years.

I also felt relief that I could trust that the crazy, mental, chaotic time bomb that had been ticking away in my head for years wasn't about to explode anytime soon now. I knew there would always be some secondary wires that would occasionally spark, but I hoped the main circuit line had finally been disarmed.

COUNSELLING

I continued on with my sessions with Norm as planned, dealing with everyday life problems as they arose, and also past issues. It's not a case of just dealing with things once and they'll be 'done and dusted'. There are always going to be things that crop up in life triggering us, and if we're complacent we automatically revert back to how we used to think and feel.

We need to count to three in our head, and in that pause become aware of our thought patterns and the associated feelings that come up with them, so we can prevent ourselves from acting on autopilot and going off track the way we always have in the past. We're now aiming to be in charge of our emotions. Our job is to pause to ensure we respond positively. The growth is in pausing *before* we react, allowing us to respond with wisdom.

I'm constantly questioning my limiting beliefs and asking myself, "Is that the *real* truth, or *my* truth? Is that my old 'stinkin' thinkin'', or could my new way of thinking be more beneficial?"

Remember the old parable, 'The Pot Roast Principle'? Generation after generation cut the ends off the pot roast before cooking it, as this was how they were taught to cook it. No one knew why until one day they asked down through the generations, as far back as great-grandma. She replied, "We had smaller pots back then." Today we have bigger pots so can cook the whole roast in one piece!

Just because something has always been done a particular way, does it still have relevance today? Just because something was once a belief, is it still applicable?

A SOBER LIFESTYLE

Very quickly, and much to my surprise, I realised I didn't need to be frightened of the unknown anymore. Sobriety was such a contrast of lifestyle from my drinking days - far at the other end of the spectrum from what I was used to. The coping mechanisms and skills I learnt in my first two years of sobriety has helped me in every area of my life, be it recovery, business, finances, health, goal setting, exercise, relationships, career, spiritual.

At the start of each counselling session we would go over what had transpired in my life between appointments, and examples of where I had used my new coping skills - where I felt I had succeeded and where I felt I acted on old 'autopilot'. What could I have done differently, acted or reacted to differently? What was I *reacting* to that I could've *responded* to instead?

We were after progress, not perfection. I'm only human, after all, and it took nearly 31 years to evolve into the 'me' that ended up going into recovery. I wasn't going to learn new ways overnight; it would take a lot of practice. Rome wasn't built in a day, and lasting changes take time.

These one-on-one counselling sessions were very valuable. I looked forward to them, even though they could be quite heavy going sometimes, never knowing what memories would be sparked or emotions would come up. I never wasted them on small, insignificant chit-chat. I'd cut right to the chase; if there was shit that needed to be dealt with I knew I needed to be fearless.

I always made sure to book the appointment times when I would have a couple of hours to myself after the session

COUNSELLING

to process what we had worked on. I found going for a long walk on the beach or in the bush was really beneficial. Or often a good session in the garden feeling the dirt through my hands. Pruning and pulling out old weeds, exerting energy and planting new life. There was lots of grieving after the sessions.

Tears would inevitably flow out of me as though my body was pushing out the old stale, stagnant energy. My garden was watered with many teardrops. It was very therapeutic. Your mind, body, heart and soul need time to be in the present moment, feeling the feelings, knowing that no matter how sad you're feeling or how long the winter is that spring will always follow. Out with the old and in with the new.

Even now I like to get out walking if I can whenever there's a good thunderstorm. It's as good as an hour of counselling. It gives me a cleansing energy boost. Better still if it's down at the beach in really gnarly weather and the waves are smashing against rocks or crashing into shore. It's not as great here on the Gold Coast of Australia where I currently live; in cooler climates it's better, all rugged up against the cold, all toasty and cosy in your 'wet weathers' and thermals with just your cheeks exposed to the elements.

A SOBER LIFESTYLE

Three Actions:

1: Book your first one-on-one counselling session.

2: Decide to be totally *Honest*, *Open* and *Willing* to new ideas. That's the **HOW**.

3: Can you identify where old beliefs could be holding you back?

Chapter 6

Withdrawals

*Some of the most beautiful rainbows
occur after the storm*
- Anon.

I was itching to get started on my new lifestyle, as though I hadn't already taken major steps just that day by seeing an AOD counsellor and clearing out all the booze and associated gear that went along with it.

I was looking forward to, albeit nervously, going to a meeting. I took out the piece of paper that Norm had given me. Damn, there wasn't an AA meeting until tomorrow night. I'd need to change my routine so I wouldn't slip back into old habits. I decided to have an early night and catch up on some much needed sleep from all the half-comatose and broken nights I'd suffered from for years.

I was also thinking about the detox process and withdrawal symptoms that were to come. Although it already felt like a lifetime, it wasn't yet 24 hours since I'd had my last drink! I was high on the honeymoon phase!

A SOBER LIFESTYLE

I went to bed prepared with plenty of water to hydrate myself, a wet facecloth for sweats, and a bucket and old towel just in case. My idea was to sleep through as much of the withdrawals as possible. Always looking for the easy route! My disease had different ideas. It wasn't long before I was tossing and turning with severe stomach cramps and trying to hold my head still at the same time from blinding, stabbing pain.

I reached for the wet facecloth to press to my forehead. It was warm in no time. I turned the cloth over and it heated up again. Oh God, where was that bucket? I tried to jump up. Just in time. But oh no, now the other end was churning. I ended up spending hours sitting on the toilet with the bucket on my lap. My head was pounding and I was exhausted.

Finally 'emptied out', I crawled back to bed and gingerly had a few sips of water. I didn't want to risk anything in my tummy being forced out again. I was hot, cold, hot, cold for the rest of the night with sleep eluding me. Then the severe itching started under my skin, like 'restless legs' but 100 times worse and all over my body.

This must be the 'electric fleas' that Norm mentioned. I tried not to scratch and instead my limbs thrashed about. My throbbing head wouldn't stop twitching. It just went on and on, all the while my stomach spasming.

I must have blacked out or nodded off at some stage because the shrilling alarm clock woke me. It felt like I'd had all of five minutes sleep, if that. I couldn't shut the alarm off quick enough. My head would only balance on my neck if I held

WITHDRAWALS

it very firm and still. I was sweating. My throat felt raw and my mouth tasted like I could only imagine the bottom of a birdcage was like. I dragged myself out of bed and as soon as my feet hit the floor I slowly steadied myself and then started to feel really cold again.

Oh God, I rushed to the toilet, dry retching, nothing was left to come up. No energy, felt faint. Went to the bathroom, splashed cold water on my face, slapped some life into my cheeks. Looked in the mirror, shouldn't have done that. I looked like shit, death warmed up. Hair all tangled and matted. No different really from any other morning, except my face was white as a ghost and not the usual sickly grey pallor, but I could actually see myself clearly now.

I turned on the shower over the bath, held on to the hand rail, started washing my hair and body, whoops, feeling very faint, sat on the bottom of the bath with the water washing over me until the faintness subsided. I stood up slowly, grabbing blindly for a towel, sat on the side of the bath to stop from falling. I patted myself dry, ever so slowly, trying to regain some energy. I brushed my teeth to get rid of the foul taste, gargling, hoiking and spitting. Charming!

The excruciating pain in my head was relentless, my movements slow and deliberate. I don't know how I got through the next couple of hours with a smile plastered on my face, getting the family off on their day.

God knows how I drove safely to drop them all off to three different school districts, but put me behind the wheel and autopilot seems to kick in. Just like all the years of driving under the influence, way above the legal and safe limit. Definitely not an intelligent plan, in hindsight. What am I talking about, was there ever any plan?

Oh God, I am so horrified to think of all the drink driving where I could've easily killed someone! Thank God that definitely a power greater than I was looking out for everyone. I don't know where all the cops were then. I was never once pulled over while driving under the influence, but many times in sobriety I've been breathalysed!

Although there's been no alcohol in my system for a very long time I still get nervous when I'm flagged over, the relentless mental chatter in my mind going, "I hope I pass, I hope I pass, oh don't be so stupid, of course you'll pass! Duh!"

Finally home again, I could collapse on the cold linoleum kitchen floor which provided a few minutes of temporary relief. Eventually I made a piece of toast and nibbled it dry, washing it down with a few sips of warmish water. So different from my normal 'Baileys on my cornflakes' breakfast of my old life. I used to kid myself it was just 'chocolate milk', after all, wasn't it?!

I certainly didn't think I'd be able to manage going into the office today. Thank God we had our own business and I could take time off when I needed to. Funny story: when I was drinking and hungover I would never take a day off, as if subconsciously I was trying to prove I was fully capable of performing like a normal-functioning adult. Not one sick day in 16 years. Now I was sober and sick as a dog!

WITHDRAWALS

Just get through this, Carol, there will be an end to it. You deserve to suffer, you've acted cruddy for so long and got away with so much. It's all part of the process you need to work through. I was a systematic person and an accounts clerk, so I knew it was just a matter of days, hours and minutes. It's all just numbers.

The thought of a 'hair of the dog' never entered my mind, thank God. It was as though alcohol never existed; all desire was removed. That in itself was a miracle. That 'Higher Power' thing again that I keep touching on.

I started to get a little bit of energy back. I couldn't go to work, there was no way I could focus on accounting and I didn't want to see anyone in the workshop either. I felt embarrassed to face the staff as I didn't know if they were aware of anything that had changed. Of course that was arse about face; I should've been embarrassed by all the 'morning after the night before' sessions, not this sober one!

I also didn't want to be alone in my home office. I was such a task-driven person but the thought of housework, vacuuming or ironing didn't exactly enthral me right now either; besides, my head was pounding and I had no energy.

I was really restless and had this urgent feeling like I needed to be around people, but where could I go? Not to family, I would only mope and have to explain myself. And I didn't want anyone worrying about me or telling me, "It's about time you got some help", or the opposite, "You don't have a problem, I drink more than you!" Yes, well …

A SOBER LIFESTYLE

Certainly not to my old drinking buddies. I knew I couldn't hang out with them anymore, and I didn't *want* to either. The only thing we had in common was drinking, and now I was sober. I couldn't think of a worse situation and I wouldn't be welcome if I wasn't 'pissing it up'. Just the smells would have me heaving and the toxicity and violence of that sort of environment was something I had happily left behind two days ago, vowing never, ever to return.

I didn't want to risk getting any visitors just turning up and bowling in the house like what happens when you work from home. I'd always encouraged it before as I was a social person and looked forward to the interaction; my back door was always open so it now would appear strange if I locked it.

Then the AOD outpatients centre flashed through my mind! I had the first of my three-weekly one-on-one appointments booked for this afternoon, but that wasn't until 1:00 p.m. It was only 10:00 a.m. I wondered if I could go in early. Mmm ...

When my counsellor and I were in the kitchen the day before he had mentioned the people that were mingling were once like me, now at all different stages of recovery and volunteering at the centre. He had explained it was like an open house where everyone was like family and supported each other. They had all seemed warm and inviting, smiling and having fun. I thought that maybe it was somewhere I could hide and relax. And they wouldn't ask me questions I didn't want to answer.

I thought it would be good to be around people who knew what I was going through, and I could be helpful, do some

WITHDRAWALS

dishes or clean the loos or something. I didn't phone up to see if I could come in just in case they said no. I just turned up and pretended I got the time wrong. Gate-crashing the alcohol and drug outpatients centre - that was a new one!

I played it by ear and read the body language. If it wasn't the 'done thing' then I could take some brochures I noticed they had. Any reading material would have been helpful to this new-found life anyway.

So off I went, and this time I wasn't bothered who saw me entering the building. That didn't mean I was going to stop and talk though either. I was on a new path and determined to do what had to be done to get well. I didn't want to talk to anyone or have to explain anything, I just didn't care if I was seen or not.

I pushed forward with tunnel vision and no eye-balling anyone. I needn't have worried, I was all wrapped up for the cold with head down and coat pulled around me, bracing against the southerly chill. There weren't many people out and about.

Once inside the building I decided to truthfully explain why I was there early. It was like once I was inside the four walls there was no need for lying or pretence anymore. The volunteers welcomed me with open arms, quite literally; there were hugs all around.

I learned the centre's motto was 'Hugs not Drugs'. Pretty cool. Many of us are so 'stroke deprived' because we've managed to push all our loved ones away over the years. There was such a feeling of warmth and security to give and receive genuine hugs.

A SOBER LIFESTYLE

We were all from different walks of life. There were men, women, gay, lesbian, pakeha (white), Maori (indigenous New Zealand), an ex-gang member. This was 1993 and I'd never really associated on a regular basis with anyone other than white, middle-class people.

Within a short space of time I felt accepted and part of a bigger whanau (family). It was really nice and pleasant; I felt more at ease than I'd ever felt with my drinking buddies, not having to watch what I said to whom in fear of retaliation or backstabbing. I was amongst real, authentic and caring souls.

Over the next few hours there was more cramping and headaches. The volunteers understood what I was going through and were at the ready with water and damp cloths when needed. They left me alone when I didn't feel like talking, but were close by like mother hens if I needed them.

The worst effects of my detox and withdrawal only lasted a few days, thank God. I do significantly remember Day 46 sober though. I woke up feeling 'different' somehow. I was struggling to put words to what it was and then I had an 'aha' moment; I actually had no hangover! I had always thought I was one of those drinkers who seldom got hangovers, but on Day 46 I realised I must have had a 16-year hangover and now the fog had finally lifted!

WITHDRAWALS

Three Actions:

1: Discuss a detox/withdrawal plan with your AOD centre or counsellor.

2: Cancel or postpone any non-urgent personal events for a few weeks.

3: Stay close to home and set up your environment as comfortably as necessary.

Chapter 7

Outpatients

Don't just talk the talk; walk the walk!

For at least the first few months, I didn't tell anyone outside of my recovery family except for my husband, where I was going and what I was doing. I needed all my energy for my sobriety, to keep myself sane and sober. I had no excess energy to expend on explaining and justifying myself or my situation.

Extended family thought it strange I wasn't drinking, so I gave the excuse of being on antihistamine medication for hayfever or something like that, or I was the sober driver. That seemed to stop any further questions. But mostly I just lay low, avoiding people and places that were going to cause undue stress and not help me in the immediate direction of my new lifestyle.

Until I could get a better understanding of my disease and a routine 'treatment' plan in place, my only socialising was within AA, the Alcohol and Drug Centre, and any occasions, events or alcohol-free parties and BBQs that

A SOBER LIFESTYLE

other recovering alcoholics hosted, either at their homes, community halls or the outpatients centre.

Fortunately for me, there happened to be an annual AA conference being held at a beautiful lake setting a few weeks into my sobriety. There would be hundreds of sober recovering alcoholics from all over the world attending. It was all very exciting, and four of us 'alkies' decided we would go. We piled into a car to make the five-hour drive to the event.

My hubby had also insisted on coming with us, as it wasn't the 'done thing' for his wife to travel off with three 'strange men' for a weekend. I was so embarrassed that he had tagged along and I wasn't 'allowed' to go away without him. One of the guys who had been in recovery way longer than me said, "Never mind, just accept he's coming; there will be a reason why that we don't know about yet."

A very wise man indeed, as halfway into the journey we had car trouble! It was the middle of winter on a pitch-black icy road when the car broke down. The other guys knew nothing about motors, but guess who was a mechanic?! *Higher Power …*

The weekend rally was a real eye-opener; everyone appeared so 'normal' to me, and full of life and energy. All the guest speakers were so relatable, all telling 'my story', or at least their own versions of it. Out of the hundreds of participants there, we would have appeared strange to the *only* 'non-AA' person. I guess it showed that *our* 'strange' was very 'normal' to us suffering with the disease of alcoholism, and this was going to be *his* wife's new normal.

OUTPATIENTS

There were lots of 'Step' sessions, lessons learnt, outdoor activities, nature walks and yummy nutritious meals, along with new friendships forged. I try to participate in as many conferences and rallies as possible. They are exciting, fun, amazing weekends where we can all be our own self, relaxed and not constantly having to fit into a round hole as the square peg that we are!

Because there is no booze involved when recovering people socialise, to prevent us from becoming bored we need to be entertained or active. This includes whether we're with *only* other recovering alcoholics, non-alcoholic sober people, or later down the track if we are socialising with drinkers or non-drinkers, i.e. everyday people.

Through the AOD centre we had great low-cost fun partaking in quiz and trivia nights, comedy skits, charades, karaoke, card and board games, sports, fundraising hangis (food cooked the traditional NZ Maori way in the ground). Funds raised would go towards hall rental, refreshments for social events, or to financially help families if their breadwinner had gone off to an Inpatients Rehab Centre.

There were so many team-building activities, resulting in personal growth, trust, self-confidence and a sense of community belonging. Heaps of fun and a new sense of self-worth, more than we had ever felt before we were sober.

Incidentally, lots of people got jobs through contacts at the AA and outpatients meetings. I had found a brand-new world, so different from the last one and incredibly precious. Sober people became my new friends. I started

A SOBER LIFESTYLE

developing sincere, rewarding and 'real' friendships with authentic, sober people. Over time, I ended up with three of the best jobs I'd ever had. New opportunities were opening up everywhere.

Lots of romances bloomed here too, but most fizzled out early. One of the unspoken 'rules' of sobriety (if you're single) is no romantic involvement for the first two years. Unfortunately, my marriage had fallen apart after returning from the weekend conference at the lake. Six weeks into sobriety and I found myself single again. I had every intention of following the silent 'rule' but hey, what can I say? You get close to people.

Learn from my experience. The 'no dating' rule is a wise piece of advice. One I wish I hadn't ignored. Oh well, lots more emotional crap to work through with my counsellor, as though I didn't already have enough material for my weekly one-on-one sessions with Norm!

There were lots of great learnings from people who had been sober longer than me. Things I wouldn't have heard if I didn't go to meetings. Nutrition advice, different vitamins and nutrients I needed, spiritual advice, wisdom and guidance from those who had been there before, shortcuts to a sane, sober lifestyle. Hints and tips of being in social environments with people who were drinking. Learning from those who 'fell off the wagon' and then came back to the meetings when sober again.

I learnt the value of routines and being active as much as possible. How physical exercise could keep my mental well-being manageable. And how to recognise the subtle signs of 'Budding' (Building Up to Drinking) and to nip things in the bud before they escalated to the danger of 'Slipping' (going back to drinking).

The disease of alcoholism is cunning, baffling and powerful. Alcoholism is a two-fold disease: a physical allergy coupled with a mental obsession. Lots of sayings that went into my 'spiritual toolbox' and were right there when I needed them; e.g. 'If you sit in the barbershop long enough you're bound to get a haircut'. Don't go to the pub or club!

Just the other day, after 26 years sober, I turned down two invites to a dinner/drinks at the pub with very good friends who happen to be social drinkers. One was for a special birthday and the other an engagement party. As much as I wanted to spend some quality time with them I couldn't think of anything more boring, and *that* little pearl of wisdom above popped into my head.

If I'd been invited to a hike or to a game of tenpin bowling or a quiz/trivia night it would have been a different story. I need to be entertained and active. I can't afford to be bored, I don't have that luxury. I learnt from those that 'slip' that boredom leads to drinking. If it's a situation I just really can't get out of I can only manage two hours maximum of socialising where the main activity is drinking.

In my old boozy days, dinner/drinks at the pub with friends would have been my favourite thing to do - I would have jumped at the chance - but my sober lifestyle is so far removed and different. I love my sober lifestyle. I can't

A SOBER LIFESTYLE

imagine my drinking lifestyle today though I do make sure I remember my last drunk. God help me never to return to it. If I keep doing what I'm doing now, I should be safe.

Sometimes I still make excuses like "I have a headache" or "I'm on hayfever medication" to get out of going to drinking events. I've missed numerous family and friends' parties and occasions over the years, but I have to look at the bigger picture. It's a small sacrifice to pay if it keeps me sober, and just as importantly, sane.

I have no intention or desire to drink, but who knows what will happen if I attend? I still remember the havoc I caused in my teens and 20s. I hurt people and nearly killed myself in the process.

Every situation is different. I don't go shouting from the rooftops "I'm a recovering alcoholic." It just makes people uncomfortable and ostracises me from them like the good (bad) old days. It's not about the booze. It's not something that can be explained to someone without the disease. It's a mental health issue more than anything. Preserving my mind. It's easier just to make an excuse and decline the invitation.

I also learned about HALT in an AA meeting. An acronym for Hungry, Angry, Lonely and Tired. I also add my own SB to HALT, making it HALTS B that I know sounds weird and only makes sense to me, but that's the process of my thought patterns. And HALTS B keeps me safe, sane and sober. I've shared this in meetings with others to help keep them safe. The S is for Serious and the B is for Bored. I try to keep all six of these in check. If my equilibrium is out of sorts I go through the six words to see what's out of kilter.

Am I hungry? Then eat. Am I angry? At what or whom? Deal with it before it turns into a resentment. Resentment is a luxury I CANNOT afford as an alcoholic. Am I lonely? Then go to a meeting or phone my sponsor. Am I tired? Then get some rest. I really have to keep a check on my seriousness and boredom too, and HALTS B is a simple way to remember this.

Sometimes it's not immediately practical to fix all six, e.g. if you're tired and at work the boss wouldn't look upon you favourably if you took a nap at your desk! Imagine if you were a pilot and took a sleep at the controls! Heaven forbid! But if I can 'tame' four out of six then that will tend to tide me over until I can get all six back in line.

We learn to weave the AA 12-Step Program into our everyday life. It is a very simple program that we alcoholics tend to over-complicate. A very *simple* program but not always *easy*. A very simple program for complicated people. A confused mind does nothing, so we need to keep things simple and manageable.

Always keep attending meetings. Wherever you are in the world there are always meetings. Wherever I am on holiday I always seek out and try to attend a meeting in a new town I visit. It's my favourite thing to do, right up there with second-hand bookshops and walking on the beach.

Even on an 11-day Pacific Island cruise I sniffed out an AA meeting in the chapel at 4:00 p.m. every day! And at that particular time of my life not so very long ago, I was in a very dysfunctional relationship that was so Boring, and I was always so Angry and full of Resentment, exceptionally Lonely, and Tired all the time as my energy was depleted, that those meetings were an absolute lifesaver for me!

You will always hear something you need to hear at a meeting. If you are asked to share, share, because someone in that meeting needs to hear what you have to say. If you don't want to go to a meeting, you *need* to go to the meeting. There is something you will hear that *you* need right now.

Don't be selfish, be there for the newcomer. They are the most important person at the meeting; if we don't attend there's nowhere for newly sober people or people still struggling with the demon drink to go. And they remind us of where we have come from. Others were there for us at our first meeting, and we need to be there for the newcomer. Pay it forward.

Whenever I'm out walking and I see a drunk in the park or a homeless person under a bridge or on a park bench, I always say to myself, "There go I, but for the Grace of God." Their face is always lowered in guilt and shame, hiding the pain of their existence in their eyes.

It takes me back to that dark and black hell-hole I was once in. I never have judgement, only compassion and empathy always. After all, I'm only one drink away from a drunk myself. I feel their emotional pain and just want to give them a hug.

OUTPATIENTS

Three Actions:

1: Attend the next outpatients meeting available.

2: Actively engage in the meeting; it helps others as well as yourself.

3: Start filling your spiritual toolbox with pearls of wisdom.

Chapter 8

Alcoholics Anonymous

*... a fellowship of men and women who have a **desire** to stop drinking ...*
- AA preamble.

This is not specifically a book about AA, although you could mistake it for that with all the references that I make. This is a book about just one woman's story of how she survived that crucial first two years sober. AA had a huge impact on my recovery and still does today. I truly believe it to be the simplest 'medicine' for my disease and I wouldn't be here today without the guidance of the 12-Step Program.

When you go along to AA you'll learn for yourself the importance of the steps, why they're worded as they are, what they mean, why they're in the particular order they are, how they work. You have to walk your own path. *Your* recovery will be different from *mine*, just as your upbringing was, your drinking career, your thought patterns and beliefs. You'll find a sponsor there, someone you can relate to who will go through the steps with you, explaining them, patiently guiding and supporting you, and also kicking your butt when you need it!

A SOBER LIFESTYLE

Even though on the one hand I was looking forward in theory to going to AA, I was certainly a bit apprehensive about going along to my first actual AA meeting. I, like every other non-alcoholic person, thought the room would be full of drunk old men. Silly me, the rooms are full of *sober* men and women! Of course, duh!

I walked in really nervous and straight away recognised a guy who was a local bank manager. I'd associated with him 10 years before when he drove the 'ice truck'. No, not the drug - actual frozen water! I was dating a fisherman in those days and used to welcome him and his crew in at the wharf at night after four or five days at sea.

The other crew members had wives and children at home so no one was available to meet them late at night. The men were truly exhausted, as it's not an easy way to 'make a crust'. They really appreciated seeing a familiar, smiling face standing on the jetty to welcome them home.

We never knew exactly what time they would be in, only an approximate ETA (estimated time arrival) they would message through the RT (radio telephone) that was hoisted up on the outside wall of my parents' house where I was living (remember, no mobile phones way back then). Jules worked for the fisheries at the time and as the 'catch' had to be transferred from the ice on the boat to ice in the truck he would also be waiting on the wharf.

It was really dark and cold at night and dangerous down there for *anyone* on their own, let alone a tiny-framed 5'2" shorty like me. I used to get a bit nervous and freaked out.

ALCOHOLICS ANONYMOUS

So Jules and I would sit in his truck chatting until the boat came in. In hindsight we were both probably drunk and over the legal driving limit, but never noticed it on each other as it would have been our normality at the time.

Many years later and back to my first AA meeting. I wasn't sure if I was in the right place, but then I saw some big banners on the wall with AA, AA, AA popping out between other words. In my peripheral vision I could see shadows of people, then that familiar face. I tried not to freak out. Jules was the first face I saw when I walked in the door.

My initial split-second thought was, "Oh shit, someone I know. How do I hightail it out of here before he recognises who I am?" I was so nervous that it hadn't actually registered that he was there for the same reason as me! Then, too late; Jules rushed over and said, "Hi, Carol, is this your first meeting? You're in the right place. Let me introduce you to another Carol."

He then introduced me to Carol, who eventually became my sponsor - the only other woman at that particular meeting. In those early days women were the minority. Thankfully more of us are now receiving the gift of recovery. Before I could scarper, the meeting was underway and it would have been embarrassing to get up and leave. I could 'do' rude, but not embarrassing with everyone looking at me.

The meeting format is similar to what you see in movies where we introduce ourselves: "Hi, I'm Carol, and I'm an alcoholic." Or addict, and some people add recovering. I always say grateful alcoholic. There's always someone who

A SOBER LIFESTYLE

'chairs' the meeting to keep it on topic and prevent one person from monopolising the floor. We're not there for a tea party, we're there to get well and stay well. Although there *is* always tea, coffee and bikkies!

Sometimes the meetings are based around a certain chapter of *The Big Book* or *'Bible'*, as we all fondly refer to the Alcoholics Anonymous manual that the founders of AA wrote in the early 1930s. We share our experiences of how that chapter relates to our everyday life today, how we each interpret it and what we've learned from it, in the hope it can help someone else.

There was an old timer, Holdy: he wore a skipper's cap and reminded me of a pissed old sea captain. He was just missing the pipe and parrot on the shoulder! Ever so slightly slurring his words he shared about his days at sea. Holdy taught me about not pre-judging people; I learned he was 20 years sober!

There was Abe from Scotland, whose thick 'Billy Connolly' brogue spoke such wisdom that everyone's breathing was so quiet so as not to miss a word. He taught me that I didn't need to yell to get people's attention. He also taught me to drive safer so as not to be such a stressed driver on our windy NZ roads! The roads he was used to in Aberdeen, Scotland were 10 times as dangerous. I just had to slow down; it wasn't a race.

There was Jack who was about my age and had been in and out of AA rooms for the past 10 years, falling in and out of sobriety, each time finding it harder to crawl back through the doors after leaving another trail of destruction behind him and another attempted suicide. It was from him I learned that the disease of alcoholism is a progressive disease. It doesn't matter when you put the bottle down, even if you pick it up years later your disease will start right back up from where it left off.

I involuntarily shivered. That was pretty scary to learn and very sobering, no pun intended! Every time he stopped drinking, Jack had to go through yet another detox and more horrid withdrawals. I knew I only had one recovery in me.

And Dory who worked the graveyard shift but also had to do the school runs every day as his wife worked crazy, irregular shifts. His sleep was continually broken just like a form of Chinese torture treatment in the war. This played havoc with his mental coping ability and he declared it was only the 12-Step Program of AA that kept him slightly sane.

I didn't know what he meant at first, but I soon came to understand and agree that we were certainly the fortunate ones. We were so grateful we had this set-of-steps 'blueprint' to keep us on the straight and narrow. How 'those people out there' (non-alcoholics) ever managed without a blueprint was something we were all in awe of. I also learned how important sleep was and to guard my mental health closely.

There were so many regular attendees and still others who came and went, some on holiday from overseas. Lots of real characters, every one of them teaching me something, leaving behind a helpful tip or a valuable life lesson. I've always believed we meet everyone for a reason, a season

A SOBER LIFESTYLE

or a lifetime. It's our job to work out which one, find the lesson and learn what we need from it.

Sometimes we shared a little about how it was in our drinking days, but mostly about the 'now' and how we got through living sober and sane in a world where we were different and often misunderstood. Sharing our experiences, strengths and hopes with each other was invaluable.

To my surprise I found myself relaxing and smiling. There were people telling 'my story'. There were a few tears, sincere compassion and loads of empathy, but mostly lots of laughing and fun! Even some 'belly' laughs and snorting! And not cocaine either! And everyone stone cold sober! A lot of firsts were happening. Fun, peace, hope, belonging. A sense of community and camaraderie.

As the weeks went by the other Carol was fondly referred to as 'Big Carol', as she was tall and added to her height with high heels, and I was referred to as 'Little Carol'. I felt accepted and like I belonged to the crowd. Just like at the AOD centre. Our normal. My tribe, my family. All my life from as far back as I could remember I had always felt like the black sheep. And I'd even overheard family members referring to me as just that! Then I started going to meetings and I found the rest of my flock! Home sweet home. There was hope for me yet.

Big Carol and I developed a real closeness, being the only regular women to attend AA at first and both being very quirky souls. She quickly became my sponsor and helped me to understand the steps and traditions of AA. Once you've been to a few different meetings you'll soon find someone who you feel comfortable enough with to ask to sponsor you. Thank goodness there are so many more women in AA now; sometimes we even outnumber the men at meetings!

One of the jobs I landed through AA was working for Carol in her fashion business. She had a popular market stall and shop that she designed and sewed clothing for. During the mornings we sat side by side in her home studio stitching up garments for her to sell in the afternoons at her shop, and weekends at the market.

We chatted about sobriety and our recovery, and listened to the local Christian radio station. It wasn't my choice of channel but she was the boss, after all. I felt really uncomfortable at first with all the GOD stuff, but once she explained that GOD is just an acronym for **G**ood **O**rderly **D**irection, everything started to make sense, and after a while I found it really interesting.

Her thoughts were when we let our EGO (and alcoholics have massive ones!) get in the way, that's when we start to get into trouble. She explained that EGO was an acronym for **E**dging **G**od **O**ut, which was us starting to stray from Good Orderly Direction. She was a great teacher, always philosophising, and I also added industrial seamstress to my resume!

Carol also had an estranged toy boy hubby who would pop by intermittently. Sometimes months would go by without her knowing where he was. He never knew either. He was a very heavily using alcoholic. Sad, frustrating, loveable, hopeless. I realised what my ex-hubby, family and close friends had had to endure for years, standing back helpless, not being able to save me from myself.

A SOBER LIFESTYLE

Funny story: Big Carol had owned a regular dress shop in town many moons ago before I ever met her in recovery. I loved her designs, but had only managed to purchase a couple of dresses over the years because most times her shop door was locked. Opening hours were the usual 9 - 5 but it could be 11:00 am or 2:00 pm and the shop would be locked and all dark inside when you peered through the window. There was never a 'closed' sign or 'back in 5 min' up on the door. And it was never regular or consistent.

Many years later I mentioned this to her one day. She explained that was in her active drinking days and if she couldn't face people or needed to sleep off a hangover she simply locked the door and turned the lights out. She would either be hiding out the back sewing, drinking or sleeping on an old couch she had. Mystery solved! We had a good laugh about it; it made complete sense to us as alcoholics!

Frustrating as hell to the customers, but they always came back. She was such an energetic and kind, quirky soul, giving exceptional service and her undivided attention when the shop *was* open. And all her designs were one of a kind; you would never see someone else in one. She taught me that as long as you haven't hurt anyone you don't need to explain or justify yourself. You don't have to answer your doorbell or your phone if you don't feel like it. It was real freedom at home; sometimes you just don't want to talk to anyone.

I continued to do what my counsellor suggested, attending three one-on-one weekly counselling sessions with him for the next three months, then scaled it back to one per week for the first two years. I also attended a women's only day group therapy session, a night-time mixed therapy session, and an education evening on the effects of alcohol (that mostly drunk drivers were sent along to from the courts as part of their sentence/rehabilitation. 95% of the attendees didn't want to be there so you had to really put your blinders on and blank them out to stop from being distracted, therefore hearing what you needed to).

The AA meetings in my hometown were Monday, Wednesday and Friday. Monday night was a nice country setting; the people were relaxed with quite a few 'old-timers'. I enjoyed the 15-minute drive out from the city to transition from my hectic daily roles of wife, mother and bookkeeper to being just Carol, the recovering alcoholic. The view from the room was an overgrown paddock with sheep lazily grazing as the sun went down. It was very relaxing to observe nature.

The Wednesday meeting I just never felt comfortable with so gave it a miss after the first few attempts. They seemed like a real 'cliquey' lot, with the meeting feeling like a Catholic church sermon, but it could have been an ideal format that worked well for the regulars. Just like all *pubs* aren't for everyone, AA meetings are no different.

Friday had always been an especially big drinking night for me, but once I was sober it was my most tired night after a long week. I didn't often feel like going out now, so if I could push myself it was a luxury to make this meeting when possible. It was a short three-minute drive from my home and held in a converted old house which gave it a warm and welcoming vibe.

A SOBER LIFESTYLE

Monday night became my 'home group' meeting. Meetings were never a chore; I looked forward to them and thought of them as my new healthy drug of choice disguised in the form of some really cool people. I hardly missed a Monday night meeting in 15 years before moving to Australia in 2009.

When I couldn't attend the odd regular one I felt disjointed and my equilibrium was out of sorts, the same as if you had missed a dose of prescribed pills for any other permanent illness.

Don't let one meeting turn you off. Attend a few times and keep searching until you find one you're comfortable at. When people are 'sharing' look for the *similarities*, not the *differences*. This was a fabulous piece of advice from my counsellor very early on in my recovery. When people are sharing their story and experiences notice the *feelings* that are the same as yours, not the *event* or *situation* that's different. Take what you need and ignore the rest.

You may be a middle-class mother 'acceptable' drunk like I was; the person sitting next to you may have been a 'brown paper bag in the park' drunk, or even a 'gutter' drunk, a lawyer, baker, wealthy celebrity or comedian, two decades younger or older, but just remember we are all the same, we all suffer from the disease of alcoholism. Shop around, give each meeting a few chances and then decide what suits you.

Another piece of advice I heard early on directed at a real sceptic was, "Take the cotton wool out of your ears and pop it in your mouth." Meaning, "God gave us two ears and one mouth so we could listen twice as much as we could speak." Also, "learn to *listen*, and listen to *learn*." That way you'll hear what you need to. Many valuable sayings will be heard in AA rooms that we can use in everyday life.

There's no cost for AA meetings. A gold coin donation is the accepted norm just to keep the rooms open and to go towards the coffee. If you're broke though don't let that stop you from coming along; no one will notice and we've all been there at one time or another.

Every time I put money in the dish at a meeting my guilt gets the better of me and I throw in extra. Back in the late 60s/early 70s when I was a young kid growing up, Dad used to take us kids to church with him on a Sunday to get us out of the house, and more than likely to give Mum a break with peace and quiet!

He would give us all five cents for when the plate was passed around the pews and had taught us to put our five cents in and take ten out, so we could all get an ice cream on the way home after Sunday school lessons! I've certainly more than paid for everyone's ice cream by now, that I'm sure to get through the pearly gates when the time comes!

A SOBER LIFESTYLE

Three Actions:

1: Be courageous and attend an AA meeting. You might just enjoy yourself.

2: Listen with both ears for parts of 'your story' being shared.

3: Be on the lookout for someone who could be a suitable sponsor for you.

Chapter 9

Group Therapy

*Who you see here and what you hear here,
let it stay here!*

These were the words written on the wall in the group therapy room at the AOD centre. It was the only way people could honestly deal with their shit. No one was going to get well if they hid all their feelings and issues. That was what had gotten us alcoholics into trouble in the first place. Stuffing our feelings down with a shitload of booze!

There's no way when we were drinking that we were going to be vulnerable and open ourselves up for the fear of being ridiculed and judged, unloved and ostracised. But in not doing so, that's exactly what we created for ourselves towards the end.

Finally, within the four walls of these rooms we were surrounded by loving, non-judgemental fellow recovering alcoholics and counsellors, where we were able to open ourselves up and spill our guts, getting all the hurt, anger, shame, guilt and ugliness out there where it could be dealt with in a safe environment.

The value of the group sessions was that by witnessing other people's issues, it could also trigger similar issues within each of us. Once one person had brought it out in the open it would give everyone else permission to spew their own demons out, where they may not have done so otherwise.

Everyone has different upbringings and therefore different family dynamics and differing perspectives. With the help of the professional counsellors we could all work through the feelings associated with our issues.

The mixed groups were my favourites as our two counsellors, Norm and Ann, were very different in their approaches; they therefore complemented each other really well, delivering just what we needed to hear. Norm was a real 'feelings' guy and Ann was straight-up no bullshit.

Norm would gently get you to open up to get past the surface feelings, peeling back the layers to get to the bottom of what you were *really* feeling. Ann would pipe up with "Get off the pity pot!" or "You can't con a con!" It could be very confronting, but you knew it was for your own good and there was a caring person behind the words. Her aim was to help us all get well.

Sometimes Norm would start the meeting off by getting us to go around the group circle, introducing ourselves and stating one word that fit how we were feeling in the present moment. Words that would often come up were sad, angry,

GROUP THERAPY

resentful, pissed off, peaceful, relaxed, calm, guilty, shameful, grounded, amongst others. Now and again someone who wouldn't feel like actively participating in the meeting and thought they could sit there quietly 'hiding' in the crowd would say "FINE." God help you if it was you. Sometimes I was the 'lucky' one!

Always one to 'shoot from the hip', Ann would fire up with, "Is that Fucked Up, Insecure, Neurotic and Emotionally Disturbed?" The group would crack up laughing, warming us up and lightening any initial nervousness.

Norm would give Ann a sideways look, sigh and shake his head, then gently continue with, "FINE's not a feeling, what's underneath the 'FINE'?"

If I was wanting to hide and not come out of my cave, acting belligerent or sulking, I'd say, "I don't know." Never one to let us off the hook, Norm would respond with, "If you knew what the feeling was, what do you think it would be?"

That would normally remind me that it would be really beneficial if I got to the bottom of what was going on for me, and that it wouldn't only help me but also others in the group. So I'd sigh, then smile, and then we could start peeling back the layers.

There was a lot of constructive feedback and also helpful role playing. Everyone comes to the group with their unique belief systems, fears and prejudices. You can also get paired off or separated into groups of four or five to work together and come to solutions. Within the dynamics of each group

A SOBER LIFESTYLE

you can never foresee what's going to happen, but you'll always come away with valuable insight into yourself, learning that your way isn't the only way, or necessarily the best way.

Everything new and different is scary at first. It's nature's way of protecting ourselves against harm. In the beginning, one-on-one counselling, AA, group therapy, role playing, being paired off with a stranger or small groups was waaaaay outside of my comfort zone or list of top activities I would choose to do. I was always fearful of looking or sounding like a fool, apprehensive of speaking up in case I came across as appearing dumb or uneducated.

After the first of everything and gaining so much value and insight into myself, others and our disease - not so much the physical effects of alcohol but more importantly the mental aspects of our 'dis-ease' - I began to look forward to every session or meeting.

I would always learn something and be able to put it into practice during the week. If you just keep going along then pretty soon the uncomfortable becomes comfortable. And I just kept reminding myself that we were all there for the same reason. No question is a dumb question. Guaranteed that if *you're* thinking it, then someone else is too. Someone needs to be the courageous one for everyone's benefit.

Sometimes I would be emotionally drained after the sessions and at other times I would come away full of energy, sorry that the meeting had ended. On the rare occasions when I couldn't be bothered going I would push myself to go anyway, just like you don't miss a dose of your medicine if you're a diabetic needing insulin. And *that* meeting would always turn out to be the one I needed the most; it could be that I needed the personal growth at the time, or quite simply just some acceptance or long overdue fun! And hugs!

There was always one woman at the centre, Mikki, who was like a mama bear and we were all her cubs. She would envelop you into her and give you the warmest, longest bear hug ever. She taught me how great a 'real' hug felt, and I learned to be the last to let go in any hugging situations thereafter, especially with kids. You never know how much your hug means to someone.

It's so beneficial to have these support groups available and the only way they can continue is if we utilise them. Often at home or work we feel either misunderstood, ostracised, pitied or fearful. We can end up withdrawing and isolating, which is no way to live and enjoy a successful and happy life. I can't stress enough how the meetings and groups are the medicine for our disease.

The fundraising we used to do to keep the doors open at the centre were some of the best TEAM building exercises I've experienced. We once had a 'hangi' fundraiser. A 'hangi' is food cooked in the ground in the traditional Maori way in an Umu (pit oven). People would come from far and wide for a hangi meal. Our hangi packs would consist of a piece of chicken, lamb and pork, with potato, kumara (sweet potato), pumpkin, onion, cabbage and gravy. Similar to an oven roast, but more tender and with a smoky flavour.

A SOBER LIFESTYLE

Everyone had a role to play and we all pre-sold an allotted amount of hangi tickets the week prior. We would get the meat donated from local farmers and butcher shops, and the veges from local farmers markets and supermarkets. We even got the tin foil (alfoil) donated that each individual hangi pack was wrapped in.

Some of us would prepare the meat and veges for our packs while others dug the hole in the ground and started the fire to prepare the 'oven'. Once the flames had burnt down and the meals were buried, they would steam away for a few hours allowing us to clean up the preparations and get ready for the 200 people we had sold tickets to, to come and collect their meals. Nothing was wasted, the vege scraps dropped off at the farmers for their pigs and chooks.

One of the volunteers knew the owners of a local fish and chip shop and had organised a donation of a huge feed for our lunch once the hangi was put in the ground. It was a really well-organised TEAM event, very morale boosting, lots of fun: kids playing together, someone always had a guitar for a sing-along. Great times. Nothing I had ever experienced outside of recovery.

Another time we put together a great night's entertainment with us all partaking in either a quiz, skits, charades or singing. We felt confident enough to look silly and get out of our comfort zone to enjoy a hilariously funny evening, sober and straight.

On lots of these occasions the kids could attend too. Different cultures mixing together that normally wouldn't have the opportunity. As there was no alcohol or drugs, we could guarantee that nothing would turn ugly; so everyone young and old could enjoy themselves for the entire time.

These social events always brought us out of our shell, and great friendships and bonds were formed. There was so much innocent fun and laughter, and with no hangover or remorse the next morning! No blackouts, no fights, no blood, no black eyes, no broken bones, no regretful hooking up, no marriages ruined, no waking up covered in vomit or pee, no police, no ambulances, no Emergency Department or mental wards! Just good, clean fun!

These are just a few of the things we did to entertain ourselves without having drink or drugs. When you find your sober tribe think of some events you can all enjoy together.

Three Actions:

1: Fully embrace the concept in your mind that group therapy is our medicine, food for the soul.

2: Get yourself along to a group therapy session.

3: Be courageous and become involved by fully immersing yourself in the dynamics of the group.

Chapter 10

Your New Social 101s

*Ping ... one jellyfish, ping ... two jellyfish, ping ...
three jellyfish ...*
- Bridget Jones movie

Our family and friends mean well, but they will never completely understand our powerful disease or complex mind. How can they? No one can ever fully understand anything if they're not going through it themselves. *We* don't know everything and we're living it every day. I've overheard people say to recovering alcoholics, "Surely you could just have one drink. One won't hurt." That's the one that does the damage! "**One's too many, a thousand's not enough**!"

We have a physical allergy and mental obsession, folks. I know you mean well, but *we* know better. Even some of the so-called professionals know less than us. I heard an admin clerk at an AOD centre once say to a stressed-out patient who was craving a drink, "Surely one won't hurt." For fuck's sake!!!

It was only rare family gatherings I went to in the first few months. I just didn't feel comfortable socialising in the

A SOBER LIFESTYLE

beginning and didn't know how to act in social situations. It was so much easier before with the 'Dutch courage' of a few G 'n' Ts or stubbies, but I didn't have the luxury of that now. It was just me on my own with nothing to hide behind. Nothing to still my nerves or mask my anxiety. Naked, but with clothes on.

There were those people who *didn't* know I was in recovery or ever had a problem with alcohol who tried to push a drink on me. There were also others who *did* know I had a problem and wasn't drinking now. Some congratulated me and thought it was great, but then acted awkward around me, asking, "Do you mind if I have a drink, will it be a problem for you?"

Sometimes they would go into a huge justification speech about why they were having a drink right now; the situation would become unbearably stressful and boring. Which of course can lead to drinking! It was just easier and safer not to attend sometimes.

An example of this happened to me at a lunch, when 20 of us were at a writers' retreat with our publishing group in Melbourne, Australia, at the start of me writing this exact book! It took every ounce of energy to smile, and breathe slowly so I could enjoy my meal. I couldn't really run away at that stage, as it was too important to finally be doing something about getting this book and message out to people like me. I was just grateful to have 26 years of sobriety and learning behind me, but it was still very uncomfortable.

YOUR NEW SOCIAL 101S

If I had chosen a different subject altogether for my first book, one that had nothing to do with sobriety, not one single person in that room would have known I was a sober alcoholic. The whole, "Do you mind if I have a drink, will it be a problem for you?" would never have come up.

The only other time I had found myself in a roomful of people who knew I was a recovering alcoholic was when *all* the other people in the room were also recovering alcoholics! This was so different; I felt very vulnerable without the safety, understanding and acceptance of my 'tribe'.

But I knew it was my purpose to write this book to help others, and if I wanted to get it out to those who really needed it, I would have to expose myself and risk being judged. The writers' retreat was a good first practice. And I must say, I actually never once felt judged; at all times I felt accepted.

That was very eye-opening and liberating for me. After all these years of being careful not to 'spill' my disease, it gave me the confidence to be myself in our globally challenged 2020, by being more open with everyday people, workmates, friends, business associates and managers. It wasn't so much that I had ever felt ashamed of my disease, I was just always wary of being judged and people not understanding me.

The majority of people have been surprised, intrigued and inspired. I have been encouraged to complete the book as soon as possible, as a lot of people who were forced into isolation because of the pandemic have come to the shocking realisation that they themselves may have a problem with alcohol. When they hear me admitting so matter-of-factly what I am and that I'm writing a book about it to help others, it becomes not so scary or taboo a subject for them. They can see the possibility of a brighter future.

At other social functions there would be the inevitable, "What would you like to drink?" Someone would urgently call out, "Oh no, Carol can't drink", or "Carol doesn't drink". It used to infuriate me inside because I could speak for myself, and I didn't appreciate someone else speaking for me, and worse still, drawing attention to me. I would try to remind myself that they were only looking out for me and thought they were doing the right thing.

I would patiently answer, "Yes, I'd love a drink. Tap water's fine, do you have ice?" Or, "I do drink, just not alcohol. What else is on offer?" Still others would avoid me entirely as they didn't know what to say or how to handle the situation. Very similar to if someone close has died, or you have been diagnosed with cancer or ended up in a wheelchair after an accident. It was so mentally exhausting and I needed all my energy for myself right now.

Just the thought of socialising without my sober tribe caused me untold anxiety. The only place I felt comfortable while I was adjusting to this new sober lifestyle was spending time with my new sober 'family'. I really had to be ruthless and stay strong to pick and choose where and with whom I would socialise now. Not just to keep myself free from the seduction of alcohol, but also to guard against the 'mind fucking' that went on between my two ears!

YOUR NEW SOCIAL 101S

I always thought of myself as an extrovert when I was drinking and friends said I came across as confident in my everyday life, but once I was sober I soon came to realise I was really quite introverted and shy. It was the bellyful of piss that gave me all the courage and confidence to be the 'belle of the ball'.

Before I RSVP to a function I visualise myself in the situation and feel the feelings that could come up. That will determine whether my mental health is strong enough to attend or not.

If I'm going to feel awkward and pressured to be a social butterfly or the centre of attention, I will make up an excuse not to attend. Being put on the spot really freaks me out, unless it's a subject or area I feel really competent in. If it's something I can't really get out of, like a work meeting, I will visualise how things could go, preparing some responses to the predictable ahead of time.

Outside of work if there are going to be any toxic, mean people present that will push my buttons, or anyone I feel inferior to, I will decline the event if at all possible. If I can get out of going to something, I will. If you had cancer you wouldn't sit with the smokers, would you?

Dinner invites or gatherings where everyone just mingles and sits around chatting, small-talking, gossiping or discussing their wine bore me to tears. Yawn. If it were an outdoor adventure walk or hike, a board games evening, quiz night, game of tennis, tenpin bowling, a play, a concert or a comedy night it was a completely different story. I was all in, excited to go. It's the same to this day; I need to be entertained or

A SOBER LIFESTYLE

be active. I can't afford to be bored. I don't have that luxury. I learned this from those that 'slip' that boredom leads to drinking. "Boredom is a luxury I can ill afford."

I set some non-negotiable rules in place for myself a long time ago to help keep me safe. But now and again I forget, or think it'll be different in this instance, or think I have this under control. *Every* time I relax one of my rules it comes back to bite me on the arse! Duh! I'll chastise myself with "You made that rule for a reason, when are you going to learn? Some rules are meant to be broken or can be bended, but not the non-negotiable ones!"

An example of some of *my* non-negotiable rules are as follows:

1. Always have my own wheels, take my own car (updated to 'make sure my Rideshare App's credit card details are current').
2. I am nobody's sober driver.
3. Sit at the end of a row or booth, and close to an exit or door. Don't ever get trapped in so I can't get out in a hurry if I need to.
4. Always have my excuses and escape route planned ahead of time.
5. Don't date heavy drinkers or active alcoholics.
6. Study menus well ahead of the meal if at all possible (more detail in the next chapter).
7. Find out beforehand who is going to be at an event so there are no surprises.

YOUR NEW SOCIAL 101S

You will work out your own rules as you go along in your sobriety. There will be ones that suit *you* and *your* lifestyle. Like I said, I've broken mine sometimes and paid for it heavily. On just one occasion I can remember breaking six out of my seven rules all at the same time! Insanity! Some would say slow learner.

I had to look within and seriously ponder over a few things, do some more work on myself and look at my lifestyle at the time. I needed to ask myself why I was suddenly allowing certain types of people to creep into my life. I was letting down my protective invisible barrier, allowing it to be penetrated by the type of people I wouldn't normally associate with. It was usually because I was either lonely, desperate for something, wanting to belong, not wanting to stand out or be different, wanting to look cool, people pleasing, not wanting to make a fuss, or afraid of being accused of being selfish or boring.

One day I noticed I was starting to feel uncomfortable and suffering 'emotional' hangovers without having drunk any alcohol. My thoughts were becoming ugly and dark again. I was getting a lot of lower lumbar back pain which I knew meant I was feeling resentful against people and situations. I was feeling like my life was out of control again. What was happening?

Then all of a sudden it dawned on me that I had stopped going to meetings and had stopped my morning ritual of my AA daily readings! Life had become really busy again! That's when the penny finally dropped. I had stopped taking my 'medicine'! I thought I was 'ten foot tall and bulletproof' and could do it all on my own again!

A SOBER LIFESTYLE

I had moved location and needed to search out another meeting. I found a 6:00 a.m. Saturday one where the rooms overlooked the marina. The sea breeze, along with inhaling the salty smells of the ocean and enjoying the beach views, sea life and boats was food for my soul. The people I met became my new 'family', and the wisdom and camaraderie I was surrounded by was just what the doctor ordered.

My books were also still packed away in boxes from the recent move, so I dug out the AA ones and started my routine daily readings again. This Saturday meeting soon became my new home group. I was reminded of the importance of 'medicine' and habits. It felt really secure being in the rooms with 'the AA banners' again. I felt safe, protected and comfortable.

Unfortunately, that meeting closed after a few months as the building was sold and the rent increase became out of reach. These things will happen, or we ourselves will move or change jobs or circumstances so are no longer able to attend our favourite meeting. When this happens we need to adjust and search out another appropriate one. Just like if you were a diabetic and the local chemist/drugstore closed and you couldn't get your insulin easily anymore, you would soon find another store.

YOUR NEW SOCIAL 101S

Three Actions:

1: Create *your* own non-negotiable rules that work for *you*.

2: Ask yourself if the people you're associating with are the right people for you.

3: Are you attending enough meetings or could you find another one to add in?

Chapter 11

Menus and Medications

*Round about the cauldron go;
in the poison'd entrails throw*
- Shakespeare's Macbeth.

Watch out for hidden alcohol in food and drinks, both in menus when eating out and at work shouts, also at friends' and family gatherings. If you haven't made the meal yourself you don't know what ingredients have gone into it. Many recipes have alcohol in them, without a thought or consideration for a recovering alcoholic. Booze comes in many disguises and can be as dangerous as a wolf in sheep's clothing!

Is there brandy in the trifle? Sherry in the fruit cake? Rum in the custard? White wine in the sauce? Champagne in the creamy chicken? Red wine in the duck? What about beer battered chips? Lemon, lime and bitters? That enticing bowl of fruit punch? What's in that pasta dish or salad dressing?

Get really good at reading menus, especially sauces, gravy, marinades and desserts. Quite often the main ingredients are on the menu and the title of the dish can give it away. If you're not sure, either ask what's in it or give it a miss and find something else.

I happen to be allergic to caffeine as well; it's a mood *and* mind-altering drug that makes my brain feel like it's rattling around in my skull! Also nuts, wheat and dairy play havoc with me in different ways, but I can always find something on the menu to suit. In fact, because I love food so much and could eat nearly everything; with all of my allergies it cuts the options down, therefore making the choice so much simpler!

If you're at Grandma's for Christmas dinner, your brother-in-law's traditional family barbeque, your nephew's 21st celebration, your sister's wedding or great niece's first birthday 'cake smashing', always ask if you're doubtful. You don't have to blurt out, "Is there alcohol in any of these dishes?" You can start by popping a few things on your plate that you know are safe and then ask something like this: "Who made the chicken dish? It looks (or smells) divine. What are the special ingredients?" You'll think of something suitable to say. It depends on who is there and if they know your history.

We feel ourselves getting trapped and don't want to risk offending people. An easy way to handle this, for example, if your nearest and dearest is pushing the alcohol-fuelled trifle on you, is to just say, "I've got a headache and anything sweet right now will bring on a migraine." Something like that shouldn't offend her and she'll most likely lay off the pressure. She might insist you take it home with you and

MENUS AND MEDICATIONS

that's okay; you can always throw it out at the earliest possible moment, or give it to a neighbour.

Lots of well-meaning people will try to tell you that cooking or heating burns off the alcohol. Well, I found this on trusty Google:

> 'After being added to food that then is baked or simmered for 15 minutes, 40 percent of the alcohol will be retained. After cooking for an hour, only about 25 percent will remain, but even after 2.5 hours of cooking, 5 percent of the alcohol will still be there.'

Of course we can't always believe everything we read on Google, but that's good enough for me. I'm not taking any chances. One thing we can be sure of is that the wine in the salad dressing is still 'raw', so the alcohol content is 100% retained!

I certainly don't need or want the *taste* either, and it's a matter of us respecting and honouring our own values and new lifestyle choices. There are also plenty of 'safe' kids' dishes.

It's not uncommon today that people are choosing to abstain from alcohol for any number of reasons, whether it be part of a health and fitness regime, taking medications for a temporary illness, fulfilling a bet with a mate or spouse, challenging themselves to 'One Year, No Beer', '#75hard', plus charity fundraisers like 'Dry July' or 'Sober October'.

If we're a recovering alcoholic we can become paranoid that we're the sober minority, but what surprised me when

A SOBER LIFESTYLE

I gave up drinking was realising how few people actually drank to excess!

I'm not one to often go to church, but I'll find myself there at rare times if I've been invited, or am attending a funeral. When it comes to communion I usually hang back in the pew because of the red wine offering. I always find myself in a bit of an anxious quandary as I weigh up either coming across as rude and disrespectful for not going forward to accept the blessing, or feeling embarrassed by having to explain why I need to decline the wine. When everyone's kneeling down at the front of the church, shoulder to shoulder, you can be easily overheard.

On two separate occasions at two different Catholic churches, both priests offered the bread, which I accepted, then when I said no thanks to the wine the priests were insistent. They didn't know my reason, so I whispered I was a recovering alcoholic, and both their responses were the same: "It's okay, it's been blessed by the Lord."

For fuck's sake! People are so ill-informed and uneducated about the grave seriousness of our disease. This is life and death, people, and could easily start someone on the slippery slope of full-out use and abuse again!

Fortunately, when in a Presbyterian church once I found myself in the same situation. As I was offered the wine, I politely declined. The pastor nodded, and then smiled, blessing me anyway before moving on to the next person. Another church I know of substitutes the red wine for Ribena juice (blackcurrant juice) for this reason, and also so kids can

MENUS AND MEDICATIONS

partake in communion. Great solution all round, covering all bases with no need for painful explanations!

Because we are not just allergic to alcohol, but *all* mood and mind-altering drugs, we need to be aware of what both OTC (over the counter) *and* prescribed stimulants and medications contain. Most mouthwashes are alcohol based, so check the fine print on the back of the bottle. I've found a great-tasting, non-toxic, alcohol-free one.

There is also alcohol in cough mixture, and codeine in pain medication. If your health 'professional' isn't understanding of your disease you need to find one who is. You have every right to change doctors, even if they've been the family GP forever.

In early sobriety it can be easy to accept what we're prescribed, without thinking of the extreme consequences. We assume the professionals know best, but not all doctors are trained the same. They've often only had a 60-minute class on the effects of alcohol in their internship; years prior. That's why it's paramount to have a specialist who understands the severity and dire effects of alcoholism, and not one who is just looking out for babies born with foetal alcohol syndrome.

A pharmacist or chemist may be able to concoct an alcohol-free cough elixir if you request it. Always check the label of cough and cold mixtures at health food shops too, as some *do* contain alcohol. I once purchased a bottle of cough syrup from the local organic store and when I arrived home went to take a spoonful and could smell alcohol. I'd missed seeing

A SOBER LIFESTYLE

on the label 'contains alcohol'. Thank God I'd poured it on a spoon first, therefore smelling the aroma, and not just chugged it straight from the bottle!

For the next two days my lower back was killing me and I soon realised I had been walking around with a huge resentment against the 'health' store for selling alcohol-laden 'medicine'. We learn that resentments are a luxury we can ill afford as an alcoholic, so I had to get over that quick smart. Lesson learnt: read ALL the fine print!

The main thing is to look after yourself and your sobriety. *It is number one, numero uno.* You will pick and choose who you tell you're a recovering alcoholic to. Only a few people know I am. It's just easier if people don't know. We don't want to be defined by our disease, and we're lucky because it's invisible so no one knows unless we tell them.

For the first three months of sobriety I took vitamin C tablets and Kyolic garlic capsules to help build up my immune system and guard against bugs and sniffles. Our major organs are severely compromised after years of alcohol abuse and the ill effects on them. Once we become 'dry' and sober our body has a chance to recover and start absorbing the goodness it craves.

I've since added in other natural remedies containing echinacea and ginseng to keep my immune system strong. In early recovery it would be a good idea to also add in a liver health supplement.

Any surplus money from my home group AA meetings was building up in an account at one of the health food shops in

MENUS AND MEDICATIONS

my hometown. If new members didn't have the funds for vitamins they could use this credit account for their vitamin C and Kyolic garlic. That could be a great idea to suggest at your home group once you find one and settle in.

Since I've become menopausal I've found some great supplements containing ginkgo biloba and Vitamin B to help with mind focus and memory as I become older. It's a stimulant-free blend containing herbs used in traditional Ayurvedic medicine. They keep me mentally sharp and on my game. We have to make sure we're not only abstaining from alcohol, but *all* mood and mind-altering prescription, non-prescription and 'party' drugs.

Three Actions:

1: Check the labels in your pantry and fridge for any devil ingredients.

2: Check your medicine chest, first aid kit and bathroom cabinet for all mood and mind-altering drugs.

3: Dispose responsibly of all you need to, ensuring you keep yourself safe.

Chapter 12

Niggles and Resentments

The dubious luxury of 'normal' men and women
- How It Works, Alcoholics Anonymous.

For ease of living and mentally coping, it's important to maintain and repair, dispose of or replace items around the home as soon as they are needed or not. This includes a button that's loose on a shirt, the lawn needs mowing, dog needs grooming, hair roots need colouring, the car needs washing. If I let all these things go, they niggle away at me and end up becoming a much bigger pain in the arse than they need to be, and in turn cause a ripple effect of needing more time and energy than I have.

If the can opener's temperamental I throw it out and buy a new one. For the sake of a few dollars it's not worth the frustration each time I want to cut the top off a tin of baked beans! I don't know what it is with me and can openers, I must have had 20 of them over the years, but the last time I struggled with one I was pleased to see in the supermarket that finally any tin food I use now comes with the option of a tear tab ring! Goodbye forever to can openers!

A SOBER LIFESTYLE

Also sorting issues with people is important to me. I'm not one to sweep things under the carpet. I need to deal with things as they come up. If there's an elephant in the room I need to address it. I need completion. If the other person won't cooperate then I have to learn to accept that and close it off. I've done what I can and I need to now let it go as I cannot harbour resentment. I don't have the luxury of resentment. I've sat in enough AA meetings to know it will send an alcoholic raving mad or back to drinking.

I find it incredibly challenging to not have completion on things. I struggle big time with it, and it can churn over and over in my mind. I will keep pushing other people for an explanation or answer, which only pushes them away and snowballs the original issue, blowing it out of all proportion. The only thing that seems to help me is by getting my 'medicine' at a meeting. It's there that I'm reminded I have to 'let it go'. One of the slogans on the walls at AA is 'Let Go and Let God'. I must let things go.

I have to accept that not everyone wants or needs closure, completion or to address issues. It may not even be an issue to them. Some people live their life by stonewalling others, or are intent on sweeping issues under the carpet and not wanting to open a 'can of worms'. They refuse to address the elephant in the room. They are happy living their life like this and I just need to accept it. But I can't afford to let things fester and build up into resentment.

This is where the Serenity Prayer (found at the end of this chapter) comes in useful, by reminding me that there are

NIGGLES AND RESENTMENTS

some things that I *can* change, and some things that I *can't*. I just have to remember to recite it to myself!

We have to be really careful to not allow people to try to manipulate and gaslight us. We beat ourselves up mentally enough on our own, questioning our sanity at times without needing any help from those that don't have our best interest at heart. While we're changing our lifestyle it can threaten the significant others in our life and they can try to sabotage our progress.

If I'm suffering mentally all I need to do is ask myself, "What Step am I not doing?" "What Step am I stuck on?" I'll mentally make my way through the 12 Steps. Quite often the answer I'm looking for is in Step One. I just need to change the word *alcohol* to another word or person's name. I'm only human, and can be very stubborn; remember we recovering alcoholics have massive egos and are always right! ... NOT! Remember EGO - **E**dging **G**od **O**ut. Remember GOD - **G**ood **O**rderly **D**irection.

Resentments corrode our life like a rust hole in a tinnie. We not only become physically ill, we become *spiritually sick* and emotionally bankrupt. The 'Serenity Prayer' is one of our most valuable tools in AA that helps big time with resentments and niggles - when I choose to remember it! It's probably the most useful tool both inside and outside of recovery. You can use it in every area of your life.

I have so many examples of resentments that if I wrote them all here I would never get this book completed! I can have 50 resentments in a day! The trick is to catch them at the time. Some I can laugh at and brush off and accept quickly, others not so easily. I try to find the gratitude in the situation.

With small things it's easy; bigger issues which usually involve a person, either something they have done or not done, said or not said, tend to take a lot longer to remember to look for the gratefulness. It's usually *my* expectations when not met that end up causing the resentment in the first place.

For an alcoholic, if we want to remain sober there are **NO** justified resentments. It always comes back to us. We can change what we can change.

We always finish off all AA and outpatients meetings with the Serenity Prayer. We form a circle, hold hands, close our eyes and say out loud together:

"God, grant me the Serenity
to accept the things I cannot change,
the Courage to change the things I can,
and the Wisdom to know the difference."

Then we end by saying, "Keep coming back, it works if you work it!"

NIGGLES AND RESENTMENTS

Three Actions:

1: What's something physical that's been niggling away in the back of your mind?

2: Take action to fix that niggle right now.

3: What resentments are you holding on to today? There will be plenty in early recovery so get yourself along to a meeting today or call your sponsor.

Chapter 13

Morning Routines and Habits

A few small daily habits when practised consistently lead to success.

Routines are extremely important, especially in times of change and uncertainty. A routine gives us predictability; predictability provides us with emotional stability. That's a lot of 'ility'! We alcoholics need routine and structure. Having the structure of regular routines to follow allows us to start the day off right and gives us a sense of purpose.

The first thing I do when I wake up, before even getting out of bed, is voice three things of which I'm grateful for:

Number one is **always** "I'm so grateful to be sober."

Number two and three can be as simple as "I'm so grateful for a comfy bed" or 'I'm so grateful for a good night's sleep." "I'm so grateful it's raining today." "I'm so grateful the sun is shining today." "I'm so grateful the dogs slept through the night without waking me." "I'm so grateful to be working today." "I'm so grateful for a day off today."

A SOBER LIFESTYLE

I once heard a fellow AA member share in a meeting she was grateful for dry sheets. And another who said he was grateful not to wake up in a mental ward anymore. And yet another say he was grateful for shoes with no holes in them. *"There go I, but for the Grace of God."* Just simple expressions of gratitude, whatever suits at that particular moment in time. "I'm so grateful to be one of the 2% to be given this gift called sobriety."

The second thing I do is scull two glasses of water to rehydrate. Once a sculler, always a sculler. I do try to sip or drink slowly, but haven't managed it automatically yet! I have to be really conscious of how I drink anything, especially hot drinks and soup. I'm always burning my tongue!

Every morning in my drinking days was pretty much the same. Wake up in a fog after broken, semi-comatose 'sleep' all night. Pounding head and cursing, "Why won't those damn birds shut up before I shoot them?!" Mouth feeling like the bottom of a birdcage, dry horrors, need water, water, water. Give me a 'hair of the dog'. Short-tempered with everyone. Crawl to the shower to wake up. Slap my sickly grey face alive. Put some nice clothes on, style the hair, paint the face mask on. Reach for the eye drops, brush teeth and tongue. Yuck!

There ... everything looks fine, nothing wrong at all. This is normal. I'm normal. No one knows any different. Wake the kids, chase them along, organise breakfast and pack lunches. Buckle them in the car and off on their day, get myself off to the office or work. That was then.

MORNING ROUTINES AND HABITS

It's funny: now as soon as I hear the birds chirping in the morning it brings a smile to my face, as I'm so grateful for the gift of sobriety and look forward to getting out of bed to start my day. They are like nature's alarm clock. I've heard other sober people say the same thing. They used to curse the noisy birds too, and now they welcome them!

The third thing I do is go for a 40 - 60 minute walk on the beach or in nature. I find the solitude and fresh air is good medicine for my mental well-being. On the odd occasion when I've had to miss this walk I feel mentally out of sorts, like I'm behind the eight ball all day long, and I have less tolerance with people and situations, allowing small niggles to get to me.

It's amazing how we see life clearly without a throbbing head and the dreaded daily hangover. My morning routine actually starts the night before. As long as I've followed my evening routine, things in the morning go pretty much to plan.

Sitting next to the dunny is my page-worn AA *Daily Reflections* book, with a reading for every day of the year. NA (Narcotics Anonymous) also have a 24 Hour book. This reading helps to set up my day in the same way that my three gratitude statements do upon awakening. I'm feeding my mind positive tools from the get-go and reinforcing an attitude of gratitude.

Depending where or with whom you're sharing a house at the time will determine where you set up your prompts and reminders. Your books might be under your pillow, in your sewing kit or tool box, in the glovebox of your car, or out in the 'man cave' or 'Sheila's shack'. The secret to success is to have them somewhere handy where you're going to be reminded daily.

I always make the bed so that at least I've accomplished success at one small thing if the rest of the day goes pear-shaped. It doesn't matter that the dogs mess it up during the day! With a routine in place I can usually breeze through my early morning on autopilot. My mental well-being is set up strong and I can cope with any 'curlies' or other people's crap that's thrown my way.

Either the weather or my grumbling tummy will determine the order of events. A warm shower, feed the dogs, a brisk walk alone at the beach or in nature with ear buds in listening to an inspirational podcast or webinar (once upon a time it was a tape deck or Sony Walkman disc player!) I try to time my walk to coincide with the sunrise; to me this signifies the gift of another precious sober day. It's like my Higher Power has sent to me the promise of a great day to come.

Followed by a nutritious breakfast, dishes soaking in the sink while I take the dogs for their 'sniff 'n' stroll'. I strive to become the person my dogs think I am, but I'm a work in progress. All they need is food, a walk, somewhere warm to sleep and human love. If there are any obstacles in front of them, they give it a good sniff, pee on it and continue past it! Life would be so simple if we took a leaf out of their book! Our canine friends can teach us so much.

MORNING ROUTINES AND HABITS

Because I'm such an active person and struggle to sit still for long, I'll make a point of sitting down to at least eat breakfast. It might only be for 10 minutes, but I'll take this opportunity to read some AA or other sobriety or spiritual material. It could be from *The Big Book, 12 Steps and 12 Traditions, Living Sober, AA Grapevine* magazine, *Al Anon*. Or any personal growth and development books, inspirational autobiographies, Anthony Robbins, Dale Carnegie, and more recently Mel Robbins. Anything positive from one of many admired and inspirational leaders.

You'll always find piles of books around my house in a dozen different areas, anywhere where I can stop, eat and read for a few moments. The toilet, bedside table, living room, breakfast nook, the deck, patio, any outdoor areas, my handbag and the car. If I have a few moments to spare or am waiting for an appointment or to pick someone up, it's a moment of luxury to fit some reading in. With the invention of Kindle and smartphones over the years I'm never without e-books and I-books.

Any vitamins or supplements I'm taking at the time will be set up in the appropriate place. The ones I take at breakfast-time are in the kitchen cutlery drawer. In your home, depending on your set-up and if there are young kids around or not, yours might be on the kitchen bench or in the overhead cupboard.

The trick to success is to put them in an area with something routine you use at the same time of day, e.g. breakfast = coffee mug, cereal plate, by the toaster or omelette pan. That way you never miss a dose. The ones I take twice a day but not necessarily with food live in the bathroom beside my toothbrush, so I remember to take them morning and night.

Cultivating an 'attitude of gratitude' is a habit I continue throughout the day, either quietly in my head or out loud if no one's around. Simple things, like "I'm so grateful for the air-con in the car". "I'm so grateful my umbrella didn't turn inside out in that strong wind". "I'm so grateful for my eyesight to see that beautiful rainbow". "I'm so grateful to always get a parking space". "I'm so grateful for a roof over my head."

If I'm feeling stressed as the day goes on, and starting to get a bit ugly up in the head with stinkin' thinkin' or resentful towards things or people, I try to pull myself up and think of something right in the present moment of which I can be grateful for. That will give me some perspective and set me back on track. Coping or not coping mentally is usually connected to whether I'm attending AA meetings or not. I need to keep taking my 'medicine'.

Three Actions:

1: Develop a morning routine.

2: Make your bed every morning.

3: What are three simple things you are grateful for right now?

Chapter 14

Evening Routines and Habits

*Habit is either the best of servants or
the worst of masters*
- Nathaniel Emmons.

My night-time routine includes feeding the dogs while I'm preparing my dinner. After I've eaten I'll wash the dishes, leaving them to drain while I take the dogs for their night walk and finish off the dishes when I get back. Dried *and* put away. I clear the bench off and wipe over the stove top, oven, fridge and microwave. I need the kitchen cleaned at night as it's a mental cue that today is nearly over, and when I start the morning off tomorrow I'm not faced with remnants of the day before.

The laundry is usually done at night so I'm not rushing around in the morning. It's more important for me to invest morning time on exercise in nature, and good nutrition.

With chores done I can then reward myself with some TV, reading, side hustle business, quiz night, writing, theatre or movie outing, or some other activity or project I'm excited about. I can relax and enjoy myself without distraction, knowing all the essentials are taken care of. It might appear that I'm too busy at night-time, but remember, we need to stay active. Sitting around doing nothing is only going to make us bored which could then lead back to drinking.

My pre-set bedtime alarm alerts me 20 minutes before bed. This is my cue to start getting ready to wind down for the night. I'll stop what I'm doing, pack things away, set up tomorrow's breakfast things depending what I'm planning on eating. I'll pop anything in the microwave overnight that needs defrosting for tomorrow night's dinner.

I always decide my meals the night before, including lunch. That way I can be sure I'll have nutritious, healthy meals and won't be stressing about what I'm going to have at the time, as it would be so easy to get takeaways and eat rubbish.

Now and again I'll cook enough for multiple meals and freeze them for those nights I'm home later and don't want to cook, or if I'm going out after dinner so don't have time for the labour-intensive routine of cooking. It's also a godsend when I have an outdoor project like gardening or painting that I'm on a mission with and need to make the most of the daylight. I can carry on until dark, knowing I don't have to stop to cook a meal. I call them my *Carolised* meals.

Friends and family have adopted the term and it's pretty cool to have something named after you! *Carolised* meals are the best! I also use these for lunches when I'm working away from home for the day. That way I can just have a protein shake and a snack for dinner knowing that I've

EVENING ROUTINES AND HABITS

already had my main meal for the day. If you're someone who loves cooking though you might really enjoy your nights creating amazing meals. That will keep you active and be your new hobby.

I also set out my clothes for the next day the night before. I'm a real planner type of person so it's easy to set up things the night before. It lessens any anguish or anxiety having to think about what to wear or what to pack in my day bag, which preserves my mental energy. I need a tidy, minimalistic, uncluttered space. The more simplicity and less clutter there is, the easier it is to clean and the less chaos there is. The less chaos in my space equals less chaos in my head.

When I'm living on my own it's so much easier to control, but when I'm living with others it can be a challenge and upset my equilibrium, which can tend to send all areas of my life into derailment if I'm not careful.

To help me stay on track I need to set up the areas and space I can control and block out the rest, like a racehorse when he puts on the blinders to focus on what's straight ahead, not getting put off course by what's around him that he doesn't need to be concerned with. Easier said than done, but with practice and setting up boundaries with people it gets more manageable.

The last habit I practise before bedtime is to take inventory of my day, which is Step 10 in AA. It simply means to think about the day you've just completed.

A SOBER LIFESTYLE

What was I most proud of today?

What wasn't I proud of?

What could I have done differently?

What could I have said differently?

Are there any negative feelings that are lingering like an emotional hangover?

Your AA sponsor can help you with this next time you see them. There's also a chapter in *Twelve Steps and Twelve Traditions*.[3]

Develop some simple routines and rituals. Create some healthy habits, and follow through consistently with them. This includes finding a good counsellor, attending AA meetings, buddying up with a sponsor to guide you through the AA 12 Steps, popping into your 'spiritual toolbox' the slogans you'll read and sayings you'll hear. Knowing the Serenity Prayer, and associating with other recovering alcoholics is all we need to stay sober and sane. Plus of course, DON'T PICK UP THE FIRST DRINK!

To live a successful sober lifestyle in the first two years is very simple. Not always easy, but very simple. During the day you have structures in place, routines to follow. Meetings to attend, books to read, work to focus on. There are many activities to keep yourself active. As long as your night-time pre-bed routine is completed and your following morning set up, at least all the little things won't keep you awake.

EVENING ROUTINES AND HABITS

Once your head hits the pillow it can be a different story though. We need to train ourselves to switch off the anxiety and there are many strategies to help with this. Mel Robbins' bestseller, *The Five Second Rule,* teaches simple systems and offers practical advice on coping with and lessening anxiety.

Sveti Williams has a great little easy read book titled, *Fix My Sleep*. We need to learn to sleep again without any mood or mind-altering drugs; this includes **NO** sleeping pills. There are many books and courses out there to help you with this.

There's a great meditation app called 'Calm', and an EFT (Emotional Freedom Therapy) tapping app by Nick Ortner called 'The Tapping Solution'. You'll find many great 'tappings' in the app including ones to aid with sleep.

As you settle into your new life you can slowly add in more good habits, routines and rituals, through goal setting, around regular exercise, sorting out your finances and setting up a budget. In early recovery though, just concentrate on developing healthy habits to get you out of bed in the morning and on purpose for your day.

A SOBER LIFESTYLE

Three Actions:

1: Develop an evening routine.

2: Take personal inventory with the help of AA's Step 10.

3: Seek out some helpful sleep practices.

[3] *Twelve Steps and Twelve Traditions* - AA Book

Chapter 15

Bills, Debt and Finances

We finally saw that the inventory should be ours, and became willing to set these matters straight
- Bill W, founder of AA.

Although we all start out in recovery *spiritually* bankrupt, we're not all *financially* bankrupt. We can be at the wealthy end of the spectrum or the destitute end, or anywhere in between. From no debt to mountains of it. Some of us leave a path of financial destruction in our wake.

Whether your business has suffered, you've lost your job, you're unemployed, the share market's crashed, or you're financially stable, take HONEST stock of where you're at. With no shame and no guilt, look at your incomings, your outgoings, your assets and your debts.

If you have more outgoing than incoming do you really need that big gas-guzzling SUV with the crippling monthly instalments? Or that jet ski that's taking up space on the driveway? Or the golf membership you never use?

A SOBER LIFESTYLE

If you have overdue bills call the creditors, explain your financial situation and ask if they would accept a payment plan from you. Tell them how much you can afford to pay each month. Most creditors are more than happy to work out something favourable for you.

The important thing is that they know what is going on. Otherwise, they will keep sending you reminder notices and eventually place your bill with a debt collector. Once this happens it's so much more difficult and will cause you undue anxiety that could have been prevented if you had spoken directly with them as soon as possible. If you're not confident to do this yourself, contact a budget advice company.

When I stopped drinking I was married, wealthy, we had two businesses, no other debt apart from a low housing mortgage. We had everything we needed. Six weeks into recovery my marriage fell apart and I found myself in the frightful situation as a single mother, jobless and homeless.

To be out job hunting again after years of self-employment was a daunting prospect. Needing to find suitable accommodation with no foreseeable income was going to prove difficult. I ended up in the short term having to rely on the government for a meagre single parent benefit (pension).

The only accommodation that I could afford at the time was to share a house with another single mother whom I didn't know well. She was the sister of a distant friend. It was soon obvious that we had totally different values and parenting techniques that made life very frustrating and

BILLS, DEBT AND FINANCES

was terribly upsetting for the children. This was all a huge adjustment for us at a time when I was also learning to adjust to my new sober life.

I had to learn to budget and ask for help in the way of charity food parcels. I'm a proud person and don't like accepting handouts without working for it. I ended up doing voluntary work at the local budget advisory office and also at the Alcohol and Drug Centre, justifying in my mind the welfare income.

A few months later I was fortunate to secure a paid admin position that became available at the alcohol centre. Even though our standard of living had significantly reduced, my two new roles were tremendously fulfilling.

Over time I managed to save up to put our own roof over our heads again, mortgage payments helped along by having our own choice of flatmates, boarders and foreign students over the years. It wasn't ideal, but a compromise I was willing to make to own our own home again (along with the bank as co-owner, of course!).

I learned from my time at Budget Advise that if you have bills that you're behind in, phone them up, as I've explained above. You'll be surprised, although most debt controllers act from the head not the heart; most creditors would rather help you than lose you as a customer. They won't be judging your fiscal prowess; any shame you might feel will only be in your own head. Eat some humble pie; don't bury your head in the sand.

Remember this: THE TRUTH WILL SET YOU FREE!

A SOBER LIFESTYLE

Three Actions:

1: Write down your true financial situation as it is today.

2: Set up a written budget (get help with this if you need to).

3: Phone up any outstanding creditors (get help with this if you need to).

Chapter 16

One Day at a Time

Keep it simple sweetie
- Albert Einstein.

If you only do **two** things in the beginning, that's all you need to start with.

1: Don't pick up that first drink!
2: Go to meetings!
The *first* will keep you sober, the *second* will keep you sane!

We are aiming for 'Progress, not Perfection'.

One day at a time. Twenty-four hours at a time. Take it one minute at a time if you need to.
60 seconds, 30 seconds, 10 seconds.

Remember, you're **NOT** alone, there are many of us out there. You just need to find your tribe; you can only progress from there.

Don't be afraid; LEAP AND THE NET WILL APPEAR!

A SOBER LIFESTYLE

Always remember your last drunk - the feelings of sadness, fear, shame, guilt, darkness, loneliness, the black hole, whatever it was for *you*. The values *you* compromised, and **KNOW** that a drink will **NEVER** make anything better.

Remember that we were born with the genetic disease of alcoholism. It could have been worse.

We *have* the disease, but we are *not* our disease. There is no shame in having the disease.

Alcoholism is a progressive disease; Cunning, Baffling and Powerful. If we start drinking again we will be right back to where we left off. We will then surely go mad and die!

The *effects* of drinking are that simple. The *steps* to a successful recovery are also simple.

We alone have to **work** our recovery, but we don't have to **walk** it alone.

Find a new favourite drink. Mine is water. It's always available.

ONE DAY AT A TIME

Three Actions:

1: Where is the next AA meeting you are going to attend?

2: Introduce yourself to the first person you see there. It may be their first meeting.

3: Look for the *similarities* in the sharing, not the *differences*.

Afterword

I didn't come this far to only come this far!
-Jesse Itzler.

Congratulations on completing *A Sober Lifestyle*. If you've come this far it means you've fully accepted that you're an alcoholic. You've implemented what you've read and learned along the way. You're now well on the way to becoming the person you always knew was inside of you.

If you need help in other areas of your life to keep it simple and manageable, you can find everything you need on Google and YouTube. Practical advice including budgeting, decluttering, exercise routines, goal setting, sleep programs and more are easily accessible and very affordable. There are many low-cost and no-cost options.

To continue with your emotional growth there are many great books, audible books, workshops and online courses that address personal development. Personal growth is a valuable and worthwhile commitment to carry on throughout your life, to stretch you to reach your maximum potential.

A SOBER LIFESTYLE

Keep on finding interests and hobbies that you've long given up or always wanted to have a go at. Get outside of your comfort zone and try something you've never considered before. Because I'm not at all an adrenaline junkie, I had no interest whatsoever in jumping out of an aeroplane, and then on my 46th birthday I decided to challenge myself and booked a tandem skydive!

It's not something I would ever attempt again, but I'm proud of myself for 'feeling the fear' and doing it anyway. Every birthday I do something 'big'. It may not be big for other people; however, if it's big for *me* that's what counts.

I had never been to the theatre before entering recovery. In my ignorance I had prejudged theatre as only being for stuffy old toffee noses! I was introduced to amateur theatre through an outpatients counsellor. She was also a part-time actress and we became really good friends. We also started working together at the alcohol centre.

In our downtime, we would practise her lines together from whichever play she was rehearsing for at the time. I would help out with ushering or serving tea and coffee at interval at the theatre, and be able to watch the finished play for free. By being **Open** to new opportunities I had so much fun. I attend plays all over the country now, it's one of my favourite things to do!

Volunteer whenever and wherever you can. Not just inside AA rooms setting up the chairs and banners, but also outside of the rooms. Think outside the box and lend a hand where you can see it's needed. At our home group AA meeting

AFTERWORD

I realised lots of members didn't have access to the AA books and other sobriety reading material. I had become treasurer of our meeting and there were funds to spare, so with the blessing of the regular members I set up a 'library' with used books I bought from Trade Me, eBay and second-hand book stores.

The library was run solely through an **H**onesty notebook. Most books came back, and those that didn't I determined that the defaulter still needed them. One guy who 'borrowed' a pocket-size version of *The Big Book* had fallen off the wagon, and it took him many sorrows and another 18 months to walk back into AA. He said he always had the book on him, and it was eventually what led him back to the rooms.

Support local causes within your communities. Take part in fun runs. For my 45th birthday I challenged myself to a charity triathlon. I hadn't swum lengths or ridden a bike since I was a teenager! The training involved months of 'nippy' early morning laps before work down at the local swimming pool, and pre-dinner bike rides after work. It certainly beat pre-dinner drinks in my old life.

I still remember the first day wondering what I'd committed myself to when I had to stop in the water three times during the first length, and was puffed before I had pedalled half a block down the street! But I was dedicated and it was for a good cause.

The more I trained, the better I became. Running through the finish line archway on the day of the triathlon was so rewarding! Once upon a time I could never have imagined this lifestyle, let alone actually enjoyed it. The secret is to keep active and be of service.

For many of us our initial issues stem from post-traumatic stress disorder that we never knew we had. In the past PTSD was something that was thought only war veterans and holocaust survivors suffered with.

Twelve months ago, with my levels of stress being 'through the roof', it was found I had the disorder, the result of a traumatic family event more than 50 years ago when I was five months in utero! During therapy for the disorder, my mental issues, perceptions and beliefs of over half a century started to make sense!

A natural progression from the PTSD work was a series of Inner Child healing workshops to provide the love, affection and attention I had needed but hadn't received as a baby from before I even came into the world. It was through no one's fault and there is no blame to be had.

I finally understood where and how my mental makeup had come about. Through many tears, regret and forgiveness I was able to 'step into others' shoes', lay to rest my shame and relax into who I am.

As alcoholics, we are a different breed and we've always been ashamed of who and what we are. Now we can fully embrace that we have a disease, and love ourselves as we are. Be kind to yourself, be gentle with yourself in this new life; but also give yourself a kick up the butt when you need it!

AFTERWORD

I truly hope this book has helped you in some way to embrace, and look forward to your new sober lifestyle. Thank you for allowing me to be a part of your journey.

Forever grateful,
Carol.

Feeling Words

Accused	Adored	Afraid	Aggravated
Alarmed	Alive	Alone	Amazed
Angry	Anxious	Appreciated	Ashamed
Astonished	Bashful	Beautiful	Bitter
Blue	Bold	Burdened	Careful
Cautious	Cross	Curious	Defensive
Delighted	Depressed	Devastated	Discouraged
Ecstatic	Embarrassed	Enchanted	Excited
Exhausted	Exhilarated	Exposed	Fearful
Fearless	Frightened	Frustrated	Furious
Glad	Gloomy	Grateful	Grief-stricken
Guilty	Happy	Haunted	Heartbroken
Helpless	Hesitant	Hopeful	Hopeless
Horrified	Hostile	Humble	Ignored
Impatient	Impressed	Inadequate	Incompetent
Incredulous	Inept	Inferior	Infuriated
Inhibited	Inquisitive	Insecure	Insignificant
Insulted	Jaded	Jolly	Jovial
Joyful	Let down	Lonely	Lost
Melancholy	Merry	Miserable	Mystified

FEELING WORDS

Nervous	Offended	Optimistic	Ornery
Outraged	Pessimistic	Pestered	Petrified
Playful	Pleased	Proud	Puzzled
Rebellious	Remorseful	Replenished	Resentful
Reserved	Resistant	Sad	Satisfied
Scorned	Shameful	Sheepish	Shocked
Sick	Solemn	Spiteful	Squashed
Startled	Stunned	Stupid	Tearful
Tender	Terrific	Testy	Thankful
Threatened	Tired	Ugly	Unaccepted
Uncomfortable		Uplifted	Used
Useful	Useless	Vengeful	Violated
Warm	Weary		

The 12 Steps of Alcoholics Anonymous

1. We admitted we were powerless over alcohol - that our lives had become unmanageable.

2. Came to believe that a Power greater than ourselves could restore us to sanity.

3. Made a decision to turn our will and our lives over to the care of God as we understood Him.

4. Made a searching and fearless moral inventory of ourselves.

5. Admitted to God, to ourselves, and to another human being the exact nature of our wrongs.

6. Were entirely ready to have God remove all these defects of character.

7. Humbly asked Him to remove our shortcomings.

THE 12 STEPS OF ALCOHOLICS ANONYMOUS

8. Made a list of all persons we had harmed, and became willing to make amends to them all.

9. Made direct amends to such people wherever possible, except when to do so would injure them or others.

10. Continued to take personal inventory and when we were wrong promptly admitted it.

11. Sought through prayer and meditation to improve our conscious contact with God as we understood Him, praying only for knowledge of His will for us and the power to carry that out.

12. Having had a spiritual awakening as the result of these steps, we tried to carry this message to alcoholics, and to practice these principles in all our affairs.

Copyright © 1952, 1953, 1981 by Alcoholics Anonymous Publishing (now known as Alcoholics Anonymous World Services, Inc.) All rights reserved.

Recommended Reading

*Not all Readers are Leaders,
but all Leaders are Readers*
 - Harry S. Truman.

AA and NA Reading:
AA Big Book
AA 12 Steps and 12 Traditions
Living Sober
Grapevine (magazine)
24 Hour Book (NA)
Daily Reflections

Further Reading:
Fix My Sleep - Sveti Williams
The Five Second Rule - Mel Robbins (plus all of her courses are invaluable)
Don't Sweat the Small Stuff - Richard Carlson, PH.D
Giant Steps - Tony Robbins
Awaken the Giant Within - Tony Robbins
The Keys to Success - Jim Rohn
Goals - Brian Tracy
Think and Grow Rich - Napoleon Hill

A SOBER LIFESTYLE

Apps:
The Tapping Solution - Nick Ortner
Calm

Google:
Unlimited meditations
Unlimited personal development content

Websites:
www.holpsy.com
www.thewellnesspoet.com
www.aa.org.au
(Search any AA country you are looking for)

Find Me Here:
Like my page *A Sober Lifestyle* and join me at *The Sober Community* private group for support, inspiration and helpful tips.

About the Author

Carol Jones is no one extraordinary; rather an ordinary baby boomer from small-town NZ. In 2008 she crossed the ditch and now calls the Gold Coast, Australia home.

She has recently embraced minimalism, choosing to live a simplistic lifestyle in a Tiny House with her two rescue dogs. Hardly a day goes by without sharing adventures with her hilarious young grandsons who live next door and think Nana lives in a super-sized cubby!

What not all of her family, friends and colleagues know is that she is also a recovering alcoholic with 27 years of successful sobriety under her belt, after destructively drinking her way through her teens and twenties until finally the day came when she said: "Enough is Enough".

Since that life-changing day in 1993 she has witnessed numerous people coming in and out of AA rooms ... abstaining from alcohol for a short time ... then falling off the wagon; once again being lured back to the liquid poison, seduced by the false hope that things will be different this time and the boozing won't get out of control.

A SOBER LIFESTYLE

Knowing the first two years are the most vital to cement the changes necessary to master a sober lifestyle, Carol realised it was time to step up and help others not only obtain sobriety, but also to maintain an ongoing sober lifestyle far beyond those first two crucial years.

Carol has now taken off her mask and knocked the invisible wall down, baring her soul, risking being ostracised by the stigma of the very misunderstood disease of alcoholism.

A Sober Lifestyle was born to give other alcoholics hope and relief to finally break free from the shackles of the cunning, baffling and powerful demon drink!

Acknowledgements

Firstly, I would like to acknowledge my daughter Cherie and my sister Wendy, who have always been my biggest cheerleaders in recovery and life. I love you to the moon and back. x

Next, I would like to extend my deepest gratitude to my counsellor 'Norm'; without you I'm positive I wouldn't be here today. You truly saved my life and my sanity on the 8th June, 1993. I am forever in your debt.

Huge hugs to everyone at NSAD and AA who were there for me when I first went into recovery. There are far too many names to mention in one short paragraph; I would need a whole 'nother book. You all know who you are, and because of you I had a whole new second family, made lots of lasting friendships and kept working the program.

Last but not least, I would like to acknowledge Natasa and Stuart Denman, and the whole team at Ultimate 48 Hour Author™. Without your encouragement, support, simple systems and professional guidance this book would still be just a jumbled collection of Post-it Notes being shuffled about like deck chairs for another 20 years.

Notes

www.ingramcontent.com/pod-product-compliance
Lightning Source LLC
Chambersburg PA
CBHW070108120526
44588CB00032B/1389